Hello, Plot.

Are You Out There?

The No-Plot Plotting Method for
Character-Driven Novels

By Lori Devoti

~~~

Interested in more information on writing?

Visit Lori's site on writing: www.howtowriteshop.com

Introduction: 99 Years I've Been Writing

So, you want to write a book.

You've read a lot of books. You've maybe even read a lot of books on writing or have taken a lot of classes on writing. Maybe you are in a critique group.

Maybe you *have* written a book or a bunch of books.

But the book you've written or want to write isn't right.

The idea was shiny and new and perfect, but as you try and get the words down around that idea, something isn't working. The idea still glows, but the reality? The reality sucks.

Congratulations! You are a writer.

When I first started writing fiction, I knew nothing. I mean really, embarrassingly little. I wrote my first manuscript completely hammering square ideas into round plot holes, forcing characters to do what I thought they were supposed to do, forcing myself to just *write the damn book*. And it was hell and I didn't know why.

Then I went to hear a writer who I liked speak. She wasn't actually there to talk about writing, but it came up. She said one word that made how little I knew perfectly clear to me. Antagonist.

My book, all 100,000 words of it was written with no antagonist.

It had other problems too, but this antagonist thing explained my major frustrations. I was trying to write a story where no one was trying to stop anyone else from doing anything. This caused problems. Sadly, though, not for my characters but for me.

Now I don't want you to get the idea that *Hello, Plot. Are You Out There?* is about antagonists. It is, but it is also about much,

much more. I tell you this story because I want to share how much you can write and still not have a story. How much you can follow conventional wisdom *Butt in chair! Just write the damn book!* and have a rambling, stringing together of words that are *not* story. That no one but your mother, if she is feeling generous, will want to read.

If you have taken enough writing classes, your writing will contain pretty words with fancy metaphors and turns of phrases, but all added they still may not be story.

Readers want story.

And you want to give it to them.

But you also want a life that doesn't involve banging your head on your desk repeatedly as you try to shoehorn a character into a plot that just doesn't fit.

You want to enjoy writing.

And that is why *Hello, Plot. Are You Out There?* exists: to help you, the storyteller, tell your stories in an as pain-free a process as possible and to make those stories sing.

About Me or Why I'm Qualified to Write This Book

As you've gathered, I'm a writer. I'm a USA Today Bestseller and award-winning author (got a cool little trophy and everything). I've been published by Harlequin, Pocket, and Kensington. I've also self-published a number of books and republished books previously published by those publishers.

I'm also a teacher and a developmental editor. The teaching has mainly been through the University of Wisconsin: Madison Department of Continuing Studies, but I also do one-on-one coaching and teaching.

Developmental editing, however, is maybe my main love. Writers and publishers send me their ideas... those shiny perfect ideas... and I tell them what is wrong with them. Well, not with the idea, but the part that comes after. The part I talk about in this book.

These aren't new writers. Many of them have written numerous books, published numerous books, but they are still there trying to get those stories to sing with an out of tune piano and a battered trombone as accompanists. They bang away and bang away, but there is no harmony. Something grates. They can sense it, but they can't pin it down and they certainly can't fix it.

With the tools in *Hello, Plot. Are You Out There?* they can and they do.

Oh, and side note... that book with no antagonist that I mentioned in the Introduction? I sold that. It was my second completed manuscript and my very first published book. Not bad for something as out of tune and broken as it was before.

Introduction Part 2 for the cheaters

Now you and I both know some of you don't want to sit here and read this whole book.

Some of you want to get right to it!

Give you the tools and let you get writing already.

If you are that person, on page 121 you will find a link to an optional PDF workbook which contains all of the forms in *Hello, Plot. Are You Out There?*

Read through it. Take it out for a spin. And then come back here when you are ready.

The rest of you, the ones who actually ate the cereal in your cereal boxes without shoving your hand down the inside first for that decoder ring... keep going. (*You are my favorites... Shh, don't tell your brother.*)

Table of Contents

Part One: Let Characters Take the Wheel

Chapter One:

When You Call My (Enneagram) Type

Now, I don't know if you thought you should be writing a character-driven plot/book, but I'm here to tell you, *You should*!

Why?

Because all stories have to be character driven or you will find yourself with that set of square pegs and round holes and nothing but your forehead to bash them together.

You don't want that.

So that is where we are going to start. With your characters. Not all. Some you can develop as you go, but at least the main two or three. And really anyone who appears enough to have any kind of arc of their own.

***

So, characters, where do we start?

Name?

Hair color?

Job?

Gender, even?

Maybe. If you know all of that, go ahead, write it down. I'll wait here.

Okay, do you have that out of your system?

Good.

Now let's get to know your characters. No, I mean really get to know them.

For this, I like to use a tool for real people, one you can use for yourself and your family if you like.

The Enneagram

The Enneagram is a method of understanding people. All people, no matter their gender, culture, religion, or political leanings, fall somewhere on the circle/within its nine types. It's a theory on personalities types that can get very detailed and intense. For character development, we don't have to wade in too deeply though, which is where my nine steps come in, but we'll get to those later...

Enneagram literally means drawing and nine. This describes the basic symbol of the Enneagram, a circle with nine points labeled (one for each type) and nine lines connecting these points.

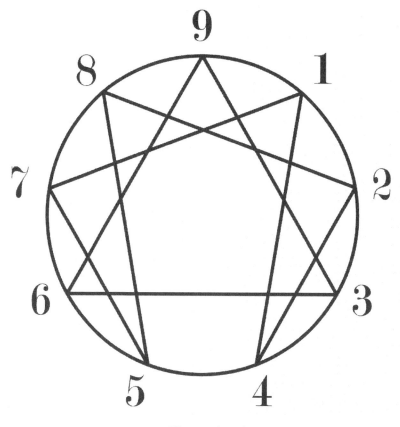

(illustration a)

Each type has a different basic view of the world, and each type is driven by different motivations and fears.

Usually, these motivations and fears are unconscious, but they push the individual in everything they do. How they see the world, how they react to it, how they want the world to see them… everything.

The beauty of the Enneagram for fiction writers is that since it is based on real people, it is a great tool to use when developing characters who readers will relate to. And, since fear and motivation are built right in, it keeps the writer from suddenly forcing a character to do something out of character. (If you follow it, of course.)

Before I give you an overview of the nine types, a couple of disclaimers. First, there is no one name for each type. Different people name each one something slightly different. Pick the term that gels with you, that helps you remember what each type is at its essence. That's what's important anyway. Second, there are no good and no bad types. All of the types have both. In Enneagram language this is usually referred to as healthy or unhealthy. I'll list some examples, as I see them, of both.

Types

One- Perfectionist, Improver, Reformer

This character has a fear of being corrupt or defective. They want to be good. They want to be so good, in fact, that they are above criticism.

This character type is often driven by a cause, something they see as more valuable than anything else. This type wants to change/improve the world (as they see the world needing improvement). They are driven by their own moral rules and can, in following those, lose sight of other things. They aren't always, though, driven by one big cause. They might instead be guided by doing the right things, being that good or proper person, being highly organized, going to school and work, being on time, being good as they see it.

They can also be... dare I say it... rigid. Which is a bit ironic considering their sense-of-self tells them they are *reasonable*. But they know how things are supposed to be and well if you know... why don't you do?

Which leads us to the trap for this type - perfection. They crave it and strive for it, sometimes at the cost of others.

When making decisions, they are ruled by the gut. They don't have to stop and think what the right choice is to make; they just go with instinct. When attacked, they will attack back. Anger is a fatal flaw for this type. Someone messed up. Someone let someone down. If showing anger doesn't fit into their idea of right/perfection, they may try to tamp it down, but it will come out somehow. Maybe as guilt for self or angry blame for someone else.

An example of an unhealthy Enneagram one is Nurse Ratchet in *One Flew Over the Cuckoo's Nest*. A healthy example is Atticus Finch from *To Kill a Mockingbird*. A more organized, driven example of a one is Hermione from the Harry Potter books and movies.

When thinking of writing a One character, think of someone who is motivated by doing the "right" thing. This could be a big thing or lots of small things. It could be something the world sees as right or something the world sees as wrong. What matters is that *the One* sees it as "right."

A Few Uses in Fiction:
-Character who takes a stand for a big cause.
 -Highly organized character who knows the "right" way things should be done.
-Anxious character who is obsessed with not doing "wrong."
-Character who pushes others to be "their best" (at healthy or unhealthy levels).
-Zealots

Two - Giver, Nurturer, Helper

This type fears being unworthy of being loved. Their basic desire is to feel loved and to be needed.

The Two is driven by their desire to help other people and be needed by these other people. A Two may serve these other people, even if it means ignoring their own needs or ignoring the needs of someone close to them who just doesn't happen to be the focus at that moment. But, never fear, point out to them that they have ignored you and they will be filled with all kinds of remorse. They just got caught up for the moment in that new shiny "other" person.

Let them make it up to you. No really... please... do...

The Two does so much for others and all they want in return is love and appreciation, but they *do* want that love and appreciation. How else will they keep the sense of self that they are loving?

The trap for a Two is obvious. They are people pleasers. They will bloody themselves against a wall to make others happy.

When facing a decision, the heart rules for them. When attacked, they will comply... go along to get along.

An example of an unhealthy Two is Annie Wilkes from *Misery* (and every controlling mother in every story ever). A healthy Two is Ray Romano from *Everybody Loves Raymond*.

When writing a Two character, think of someone who is motivated by helping others. They want to help other people, not because it is "right" but because they just have to... it's who they are. This "help" though is in the eye of the Two, not necessarily in the eye of the receiver.

A Few Uses in Fiction:

-Parent who does "everything" for their "ungrateful" child.

-Teachers, counselors, or nurses who are truly fulfilled by helping others.

-Obsessive fan or stalker

-People Pleaser who can't say "no"

-Master Manipulator (Two with Three-wing. Read on for information on wings.)

Three – Achiever, Succeeder

A Three has a fear of public disgrace. They need to feel valuable and worthwhile.

Threes are worker bees, but they aren't happy just being a member of the hive. They want to be recognized for that work. They want to be seen as the best worker bee in the history of worker bees. They are quick learners and productive. They keep the hive buzzing... as in on track.

Because of their dedication, they are usually on their way to high places, if they aren't already there.

And they love goals! Setting them. Striving for them. Blasting through them.

Because Threes want to get attention and be admired, they can resort to deception to get that attention/admiration if their drive isn't achieving a reality that brings that recognition along naturally.

They see themselves as outstanding, as in standing out from the crowd, but because they also love to get to their goals fast, they can get tripped up by this desire for efficiency. This will then lead them back to the need for deception and so forth and so on...

With decisions, they are ruled by the heart, but if attacked or challenged, they will fight back. No shrinking violet here.

An example of an unhealthy Three is Tom Ripley in *The Talented Mr. Ripley.* A *gray* Three is Scarlett O'Hara from *Gone With the Wind.*

When writing a Three character, think of someone who wants to appear successful. They are willing to work for this success (as they see success), but if true success is unattainable, they may cheat to get it or settle for just the appearance of success.

A Few Uses in Fiction:
-Co-worker who steals others' ideas
-Hard-working charismatic CEO
-Straight A student who works hard to keep grades up
-Straight A student who abuses medications for focus, etc. to maintain GPA, activities, etc.
-Narcissist
-Con Man/Woman

Four – Romantic, Individualist

The Four on the Enneagram fears being without a personal identity or significance. Being one of the cogs, indistinguishable from the others, is their personal nightmare. They want to "find themselves" and their significance in the world.

Fours are dreamers, artistic and romantic. They can be compassionate to others, but also depressed and self-absorbed.

They are willing to suffer for love. They also have flair and like to have a distinct personal style.

Fours want to express themselves authentically. They want to be surrounded by beauty and live life in certain "moods." Some may feel they need a "rescuer" to help them with this.

Their major flaw is envy. Not because they are greedy, but because they can suffer from self-doubt and low self-esteem.

They see themselves as unique, and this brings them to their trap which is elitism. Being normal is not good. They must be unique.

When faced with a decision, the heart rules for them, and if attacked they will retreat.

An example of an unhealthy Four is Blanche DuBois in *A Streetcar Named Desire*. A healthy Four is Rick Blaine in *Casablanca*.

When writing a Four character, think of someone for whom self-expression and personal identity are of utmost importance. They want to be "authentic." They don't necessarily want to stand out from the crowd, but if being true to themselves means they will, then they will.

A Few Uses in Fiction:
-High school loner
-Creative genius
-Bitter adult who hold onto past wrongs
-Romantic who is in love with "being in love"

Five – Observer, Thinker

The Enneagram Five fears being useless, incompetent, or incapable. They want to be capable and competent, not just *be seen* as capable and competent. They want *to be…*

Fives are gatherers of information and observations. They are the person in the back of the room watching and remembering whatever they have seen. They make great researchers and investigators. You will see them as the eccentric detective in fiction quite often. They are also very objective in their views of what they learn and love to turn problems over and over, looking for new solutions someone else may have missed.

Because of this objectivity, they can also be socially awkward and just not know how, or want, to relate to other humans. They can be so sure of their rightness that they become arrogant and even obnoxious.

A Five wants to possess knowledge and have everything figured out. Their nightmare is being wrong. Their vice is greed, but most often for knowledge and privacy, not wealth.

They see themselves as perceptive and their trap is their desire to know all/acquire all knowledge.

When making a decision, they are most certainly ruled by the head and logic. If challenged or attacked they will withdraw.

An example of an unhealthy Five is Dr. Gregory House from *House M.D.*. (Although during parts of the show he is high-functioning.) An example of a healthy (mostly healthy) Five is Sherlock Holmes from *A Study in Scarlett, Sherlock*, etc..

When writing a Five character, think of someone who likes to gather information and solve problems. They are independent thinkers who may be a bit (or a lot) arrogant about their abilities. They will be objective, but maybe to the point of seeming cold.

A Few Uses in Fiction:
-Eccentric genius
-Detective
-Dedicated researcher
-Reporter
-Recluse

Six – Skeptic, Trouble-Shooter, Pessimist, Loyalist

The Enneagram Six fears being without support or guidance. Because they are born skeptics, trust, even in their own instincts, doesn't come easy. They need to feel supported in their choices to feel safe.

Sixes tend to be anxious… Am I doing the right thing? Can I really trust this person? Can I really trust these *facts*? For them, our world is a dangerous one. They may run to this danger or away from it. Fight or flight? It depends on the Six. A "counterphobic" Six will fight. A "phobic" Six will flee.

Along with being worriers, Sixes can also be extremely loyal. Once you have their trust, you have it. They can be endearing and lovable, dedicated to both individuals and movements. They can also, though, be panicky and volatile, and lash out irrationally.

Sixes see themselves as reliable, and their trap is security. They need to feel safe.

When faced with a decision, they use their heads. When challenged or attacked, they will comply.

An example of a phobic Six is Woody Allen in pretty much every movie he was in. Jerry Seinfeld and George Costanza from *The Seinfeld Show* are both healthy Sixes, mainly in the phobic range. Alex Karev in *Grey's Anatomy* is a healthy counterphobic Six.

When writing a Six character, think of someone who doesn't trust easily. They are skeptical of people, facts, etc. However, once past that skepticism, they are extremely loyal.

A Few Uses in Fiction:
-Detective side-kick
-Neurotic hermit
-Over-protective parent
-Blind follower, afraid to break away from group/leader and think on own
-Loyal friend

Seven – Adventurer, Visionary, Enthusiast

The Enneagram Seven fears being deprived or trapped, could be in pain, a situation, a relationship, etc. A Seven needs to be free to fly, to chase the next big adventure, to have fun. Their basic desire is to be satisfied and fulfilled.

Sevens are performers in the stage sense of the word. They are the life of the party, filled with joy, optimism, and curiosity. They thrive on change. They can, though, take this too far. They can become addicted to the highs of life: sex, excitement, and adventure. They can also get bored and feel trapped when they are "stuck" in one place or situation too long.

Sevens want to be free and happy. They want to be satisfied and fulfilled and are on the hunt for this fulfillment all the time. This makes them open to the sin of gluttony.

They see themselves as enthusiastic, the world's cheerleaders, and their trap is idealism.

When faced with a decision they use their heads, and when challenged they comply.

An example of an unhealthy Seven is Daniel Cleaver in *Bridget Jones Diary* or again, Hugh Grant in about anything. Holly Golightly in *Breakfast at Tiffany's* is a healthy Seven and then there's Peter Pan… you decide if he is healthy or not…

When writing a Seven character, think of someone who is optimistic and just wants to be happy. They look for opportunities to do that. Because of their zest for life, others will be attracted to them. They can though be fickle and become bored easily or just have too many thoughts/opportunities happening in their minds at once to latch onto just one.

A Few Uses in Fiction:
-Playboy
-Belle of the Ball
-Ditz
-Cheerleader (literally or of the group)
-Renaissance Man/Woman

Eight – Leader, Boss, Challenger

The Enneagram Eight fears being controlled or violated. Their most basic desire is to protect themselves.

Eights can be magnanimous and courageous. They have can-do attitudes and are natural leaders, but they can also be ruthless and dictatorial, feel omnipotent and be vengeful. They are preoccupied with power but can be fierce and loyal friends. They are who you want with you in a fight, and they have a love for the underdog and innocent.

Eights want to be seen as self-reliant and important. Their flaw is their lust for power, activity, challenge, purpose, etc..

They see themselves as strong and their traps are arrogance, vengeance, and a need for justice.

When faced with a decision, they go with their gut. If challenged they respond with aggression.

An example of a healthy Eight is Rhett Butler in *Gone With the Wind*. An unhealthy Eight is Michael Corleone in *The Godfather*.

When writing an Eight character, think of someone who is or wants to be in charge, but also has a soft spot for those they feel need their protection. They are not afraid of a fight.

A Few Uses in Fiction:
-Mob Boss
-General (or any military leader)
-Domineering Parent
-CEO (who leads via a strong will)

Nine – Peacemaker, Mediator

The Enneagram Nine fears loss and separation. The Nine wants peace of mind and wholeness.

Nines are patient and good-natured, optimistic, and supportive. They make a great listening board and friend. They can also though be neglectful, stubborn, and repressed.

Nines want harmony and resist what will upset them. They avoid conflict at all costs. This leads to their flaw which is sloth. Better to do nothing than to make waves.

They see themselves, though, as whole and Zen, but are vulnerable to falling into the trap of indecision.

When faced with a decision, they will go with their gut, but faced with a challenge, they will withdraw.

An example of an unhealthy Nine is Professor Humbert Humbert from *Lolita*. A healthy example of a Nine is Dorothy from *The Wizard of Oz*.

When writing a Nine character, think of someone who is easy to talk to, mainly because they don't openly disagree with what is being said. This doesn't, however, mean they actually agree.

A Few Uses in Fiction:
-Reluctant hero/heroine
-Sounding board best friend
-Couch Potato/Living in Parent's Basement
-Negotiating Middle Man (Counsellor, Hostage Negotiator, Diplomat)

These are the basics of the Nine Types and all you need to know if you use my Nine Steps to Building Characters. However, there is more. *A lot* more. You can spend years down the rabbit hole that is the Enneagram. It might even become a passion all on its own.

I don't want to spend too much more time on it here, because we are here to write a book! But, just a few more details for those of you interested… if you aren't, move on… no penalty for that at all.

Subtypes

What I listed before were the basic Nine Types of the Enneagram. People in each of these also have "instinctual subtypes." These three subtypes are found in all of the Nine Types and are derived from that person's basic survival strategy or instinct. They are what drives that person's passions. When you combine these three subtypes with the Nine main types, you have 27 overall variations. (9 x 3 = 27) This explains partially why different people with the same basic type can be so different from each other. (There are more reasons to come, but let's stick with subtypes now.)

These three are:
   Self-preservation
   Social
   One-to-One

A self-preservation subtype is driven by… you guessed it… self-preservation. This means they worry about the basics such as food, shelter, clothing. These things make them feel secure.

A social subtype needs to belong to a bigger group and their relationship to that group is very important to them. It can become part of their own identity.

A one-to-one (sometimes called sexual) subtype needs close relationships. Those one-on-one friendships and sexual relationships are most important to them.

Let's take a look at the types and see how they change with the different subtypes.

Type 1: The Perfectionist, Improver, Reformer

A Type 1 with a self-preservation subtype worries. The engine light came on in their car. They should get that fixed. Now, maybe sooner. New baby on the way? Expect every electrical outlet to be covered before the mother-to-be is out of her first trimester. **Potential Character: Over-achiever**

A Type 1 with a social subtype likes groups with rules. Rules they can learn and live. If forced to choose between a new fact and a long-trusted group rule, they may ditch the fact. But if the group rule starts to fight with a long-held personal principle? Well, the principle will win that battle. **Potential Character: Whistle Blower** (but in protection of the group against a betrayer)

A Type 1 with a one-to-one subtype sees the person with whom they have a close personal relationship as close to perfection. So much so the One may push that person to do that *one more thing* to make them *actually* perfect, or they may get jealous because obviously this person is so perfect… or so close to perfect… how can the One hope to keep them happy? **Potential Character: Stage Mom**

Type 2: The Giver, Nurturer, Helper

A Type 2 with a self-preservation subtype may reward themselves with "treats" for all they do for others and feel free to spend dollars they may or may not have both for self-reward and to advance their efforts to help others. They are great at doing for others, but also expect recognition and thanks for this "doing." They will notice when they don't get that thank you card. **Potential Character: Doting Aunt**

A Type 2 with a social subtype finds fulfillment through helping others in a group they value. They will value their relationships with the "right people" in the group more than recognition for their own accomplishments. **Potential Character: Sidekick**

A Type 2 with a one-to-one subtype excel at making friends and they will probably try to make as many individual connections as possible. They are great listeners and talented at remembering things valued by their friends, such as movies, food, or authors. This friendship though, may not be particularly deep. Better to have a lot of options than to be nailed down to one choice. Plus, then they would miss out on the fun of the chase. **Potential Character: Heart-sick Teen** (longing for out of reach love match)

Type 3: The Achiever, Succeeder

A Type 3 with a self-preservation subtype works hard for concrete rewards such as a nice house, car, or the corner office. **Potential Character: Keeping Up with the Joneses**

A Type 3 with a social subtype sees success in who they know. They work hard to get power socially and want to "know the right people." **Potential Character: Politician**

A Type 3 with a one-to-one subtype tends to use their own physical appeal to gauge success, likely with an emphasis on what is seen as attractive for their gender. **Potential Character: Big Man On Campus**

Type 4: The Romantic, Individualist

A Type 4 with a self-preservation subtype are dauntless. They can be aggressive in their quest for identity and take life-endangering risks in their efforts to establish it. **Potential Character: Daredevil** (with dramatic flair)

A Type 4 with a social subtype is very sensitive to not being part of the group. If a Four is brought up in a group that has as part of its core beliefs something that conflicts with something important or basic to the Four, this can be challenging for the Four. A social subtype Four needs to find their "tribe" perhaps more than any other type. **Potential Character: Truth-Teller**

(possibly the bitter truth as character struggles to merge own identity with group)

A Type 1 with a one-to-one subtype values love and relationships. They can become competitive in their efforts to find and maintain them. They are also more likely to believe in "soul mates," the one true person for them. **Potential Character: Star-Crossed Lover**

Type 5: The Observer or Thinker

A Type 5 with a self-preservation subtype wants things. Things make him feel safe. He might become a hoarder. **Potential Character: Collector** (antiques, sports memorabilia, etc.)

A Type 5 with a social subtype will want to learn everything there is to know about his chosen group. He'll know the history, the handshake, have the T-shirts, etc. His Fiveness though will probably keep him from being a social member of the tribe. He'll know all about the group but won't necessarily be part of the emotion surrounding it. **Potential Character: Super Fan**

A Type 5 with a one-to-one subtype will gather all his things and knowledge as fives love to do, but he will only trust a select few with whom to share. His information is important, and you must be one of the trusted few to be entrusted with it. **Potential Character: Detective**

Type 6: The Sceptic, Trouble-Shooter, Pessimist, Loyalist

A Type 6 with a self-preservation subtype finds safety in their friends. They value the feeling that they can be themselves around this select group and let go of their worry for a bit.

Charm and a self-deprecating sense of humor help them build these friendships. **Potential Character: Miss Congeniality**

A Type 6 with a social subtype finds safety from associating with a larger group. They might even be suspicious of people not in this group while intensely loyal to the members. They can idealize the leader as long as that leader maintains their trust. However, if that leader fails the group or turns against it himself, the social Six will just as quickly turn on him. **Potential Character: Cult Follower**

A Type 6 with a one-to-one subtype may try to appear strong and brave, or he might focus on beauty, his own or creating it around him to gain close relationships. He will try to use willpower to tamp down his fear. **Potential Character: Activist**

Type 7: The Adventurer, Visionary, Enthusiast

A Type 7 with a self-preservation subtype looks for people who share the same interests and values as they do. They like being with those people, but they also like planning for being with these people. **Potential Character: Hostess with the Mostess**

A Type 7 with a social subtype are enthusiastic members of the group, as long as the group doesn't bog things down with unnecessary rules, or "classes" where some members are in the Seven's mind unfairly valued more than others. If or when these things happen, the Seven is out. **Potential Character: Charismatic Leader... who possibly rebels.**

A Type 7 with a one-to-one subtype uses his personal charm to lead others into uncharted territory. This Seven is excited about new ideas and new relationships, and he shares it with others. Sevens being Sevens though, the attraction (from the Seven's point of view) may grow boring, causing him to move on to the next new intriguing person. **Potential Character: Love 'em and Leave 'em**

Type 8: The Leader, Boss, Challenger

A Type 8 with a self-preservation subtype is protective of friends and family and sees things as a way to provide that protection. They want to be tough and prepared for whatever comes their way. **Potential Character: End of World Prepper**

A Type 8 with a social subtype strongly associates themselves with their chosen group, usually taking on a leadership role. They will embrace the purpose of the group and be loyal to those who are true to it. However, those who threaten the group will fall victim to this Eight's anger. **Potential Character: Mob Boss**

A Type 8 with a one-to-one subtype likes honesty. They are looking for someone they can trust enough to give that person power over them, although in their perfect relationship they would be boss. They also though value strength in their partner and like a partner who will call them out if they mess up. **Potential Character: CEO**

Type 9: The Peacemaker, Mediator

A Type 9 with a self-preservation subtype seeks out physical comfort which they find through food and material items. They value what is tried and true to them: recipes, movies, vacation spots, etc. **Potential Character: Kid Living in Parents' Basement.**

A Type 9 with a social subtype excel at blending. They know how to dress and how to act to be part of the group and they don't mind doing it as long as others don't expect too much else out of them. Even then, the Nine won't complain or throw a fit.

He will just quietly back away until the expectations are dropped. **Potential Character: The Follower**

A Type 9 with a one-to-one subtype is looking for the one perfect person and may see that perfection when it doesn't exist. They will ignore issues that would cause others to walk away. **Potential Character: Henpecked Husband/Badgered Wife**

Can you see the subtle differences in these? Can you think of a character that fits one of these subtypes?

Wings

The next reason two people of the same type may be different from each other is wings.

If you look back at the basic diagram you will see that every type is between two other types because, duh… a circle.

The types on each side of the person's main types have the potential to be wings. Your main type is what dominates/drives your personality, but most likely one of the types on either side have an effect too, maybe even both. This is the other side of your personality or your wing. You will see this described as an 8w9. That's a person whose main personality is Type 8, but they show some 9 characteristics too.

For the purposes of writing, looking at characters with their wings considered may help you pen them down more exactly.

Here's a brief overview of each for you to consider.

Type 1w9 – The Idealist

Ones with a nine-wing are less likely to assert their judgments on others, and due to the nine's fear of conflict, they take on the role of quiet judgers. They tend to have a better handle on their emotions, taking longer to express their rage. They may come off as dry, strict, and aloof. Ones with a nine-wing are also less motivated towards advancing their chosen cause or mission than ones with a two-wing.

Type 1w2 – The Advocate

Ones with a two-wing are more likely to dismiss their frustrations with people who fail to live up to their harsh standards. However, when you don't do things their way, they will feel freer to tell you what you're doing wrong. Ones with a two-wing are more driven and active when it comes to changing the world into what they believe it should be.

Type 2w1 – The Altruist

Twos with a one-wing are more emotionally controlled and serious than twos with a three-wing. They lock strong emotions and impulsivity away in an effort to remain polite. The blend of the two's desire to give and the one's strong principles can result in the two's affection becoming more selective, diverting towards people or goals that support their morals.

Type 2w3 – The Hostess

Twos with a three-wing are more outgoing, emotional, and concerned with their appearance than other twos. They enjoy committing themselves to helping as many people as they can and are more at ease in the spotlight. Twos with a three-wing are more prone to having emotional outbursts and being manipulative/deceitful of others.

Type 3w2 – The Charmer

As the name indicates, threes with a two-wing are optimistic charmers. Much like a seven, they want to be happy. They also, though, want to help others be happy. They have a need to be liked and spend time working on being irresistible to others. They live on a stage of sorts, performing a role and will work hard to maintain/improve whatever image they have designed for themselves. Their desire for attention, however, doesn't mean they want close relationships. Intimacy can make them uncomfortable, and their goal-driven need to improve may wear on them.

Type 3w4 – The Professional

Threes with a four-wing want to be seen as exceptional but are more comfortable with being different or outside accepted norms. They look at what they have done themselves and find competition within themselves. They will work hard to be the best and to control how they are represented by others. If they feel underappreciated they might blame the other person or group for not being knowledgeable enough to understand the 3w4's talent/value.

Type 4w3 – The Individual

Fours with a three-wing enjoy being distinct individuals. Whatever their "thing" is they will present it in a creative and unique way. They are outgoing and approach the world with humor and flair. They can also, though, be melodramatic and project romantic images onto others that are only creations of the 4w3's mind.

Type 4w5 – The Bohemian

Fours with a five-wing thrive on not fitting in. They see themselves as unique and are more likely than not to turn their noses up at tradition or "going along with the crowd." However, since fours with a five-wing spurn convention and conventional wisdom, it can be hard for them to get the appreciation for their creations and uniqueness that they also desire. How can you celebrate acceptance from the masses when your identity is tied to not being part of them?

Type 5w4 – The Challenger

Fives with a four-wing like to imagine a wide range of theories, often delving into the realm of "what could be" rather than what is. They tend to question the world around them, considering the strength of old theories and new ones. The four-wing encourages them to come up with original ideas and distinguish themselves, rather than just simply excelling in their chosen field. They are more social than fives with a six-wing, while simultaneously being more introverted and emotional.

Type 5w6 – The Problem Solver

Fives with a six-wing are skeptics who don't trust "common wisdom." Because of this, they question what others accept. Their questioning, combined with an ability to reason, allow them to see "better alternatives" to many things. Fives with six-wings, however, may feel and act awkward around other people. This doesn't though mean they will not find success. Many of today's most acclaimed innovators fit this type.

Type 6w5 – The Defender

Sixes with a five-wing are more independent and less social than sixes with a seven-wing. They prefer to wait to be approached and then vet potential friends, versus searching out new allies. This forces them to be more independent, as they end up leaning on themselves to comfort their anxieties instead of others. Sixes with a five-wing tend to have strong ethical, moral, or political opinions. They usually feel particularly drawn to those they see as disadvantaged and speak out passionately for the issues they're committed to.

Type 6w7 – The Buddy

Sixes with a seven-wing have an overt desire to be liked and accepted. They are more social and depend on the support of others to comfort their fears. They tend to search out friendships, unlike a six with a five-wing who waits to be approached. Their seven-wing's wealth of ideas allows them to see all the possible ways things could go wrong, typically filling them with anxiety. They will use distractions to avoid their anxieties due to their seven-wing, in addition to their close friendships.

Type 7w6 – The Entertainer

Sevens with a six-wing make great entertainers. Many comedians fit this type. They are endearing and funny, while also pulling on the less secure aspects of a six and being nervous. They are both charming and practical but can feel guilty and be self-destructive. Sevens with a six-wing can have trouble showing anger, but don't like being told what to do and may try to get around authority or challenge it.

Type 7w8 – The Realist

Sevens with an eight-wing embrace life, but may do so with an edge of hard, even callous reality. They want to be seen as a success but are willing to rebel against others' opinions. They are willing to jump into the fray to defend someone they care about, enjoy living life, and want to share what they love with others. They can be impatient and even aggressive, especially when things don't turn out as they expected them to. They can also be hypocritical perfectionists, criticizing others for things they themselves do as well.

Type 8w7 – The Maverick

Eights with a seven-wing take on the mentality of "the best defense is a good offense." They tend to be more outwardly aggressive and are more likely to attack first. Their seven-wing gives them an appreciation for the strategic/tactics of arguing and winning fights. They can come off as more arrogant and obviously confident than an eight with a nine-wing. They can also be more vulnerable to taking high risks and self-destruction.

Type 8w9 – The Bear

Eights with a nine-wing are quietly confident and appear as if they're free of self-doubts. Unlike the eight with a seven-wing, the nine-wing won't search out fights or randomly push on others to assert dominance. Eights with a nine-wing tend to only pursue fights when they need something or when someone else makes the first move. Even when angry, they won't throw everything they have at you. They prefer to endure your attacks and slowly push their weight on you until you back down.

Type 9w8 – The Referee

Nines with an eight-wing are less motivated than nines with a one-wing. When angry they maintain a calm exterior, but once they can't handle it anymore they suddenly explode in rage. After their explosion, they tend to return to their calm and controlled demeanor. They also tend to mistake being assertive with being rude. During arguments, they may "blow off steam" through their "assertive" comments in an effort to avoid losing control of their temper.

Type 9w1 – The Dreamer

Nines with a one-wing tend to express their anger by becoming critical of others and even at times bitchy, opposed to nines with an eight-wing who will suddenly explode. Nines with a one-wing set high expectations for themselves in all aspects of their lives. When they don't rise to meet these expectations, it results in the nine being very hard on themselves. This mentality makes them more sensitive to criticism.

Under Stress or Security

Look back at the diagram again. See the lines? See how different types are connected to each other by these lines? Those are how the different types react when feeling secure or stressed. I like to use this for characters because it can explain contradictions many great characters have. Put a character under great stress and they may do something that seems out of character, but is it?

Not necessarily.

It may (and hopefully will when you are done with this book) be completely normal for them. And, because it is based on the Enneagram and real people, not seem out of character at all to your readers, just a nice thrill of *I didn't see that coming… but it makes sense and I like it…*

So….

Type 1: Perfectionist, Improver, Reformer
  Under Stress – Type 4
  Feeling Secure – Type 7

Type 2: Giver, Nurturer, Helper
  Under Stress – Type 8
  Feeling Secure – Type 4

Type 3: Achiever, Succeeder
  Under Stress – Type 9
  Feeling Secure – Type 6

Type 4: Romantic, Individualist
  Under Stress – Type 2
  Feeling Secure – Type 1

Type 5: Observer, Thinker
  Under Stress – Type 7
  Feeling Secure – Type 8

Type 6: Sceptic, Trouble-Shooter, Pessimist, Loyalist
  Under Stress – Type 3

Feeling Secure – Type 9

Type 7: Adventurer, Visionary, Enthusiast
Under Stress – Type 1
Feeling Secure – Type 5

Type 8: Leader, Boss, Challenger
Under Stress – Type 5
Feeling Secure – Type 2

Type 9: Peacemaker, Mediator
Under Stress – Type 6
Feeling Secure – Type 3

You will notice there is overlap. So, a Seven feeling safe and secure is going to look a lot like a Five who is stressed. This can make it difficult to type someone unless you have seen them in a number of situations, but if you type yourself, I think you will see the truth of this. You may realize you aren't the type you initially thought you were at all. That type is just where you are hanging out when you a feeling secure, etc.

And the same can be said for your characters. So if you are ever in a situation where you are trying to decide how your character should react to some event, come back and check this. It just might give you a new idea to get you jump-started.

Other

There are other aspects to the Enneagram too. A couple I covered in the Type descriptions: how a type reacts to a threat and how they make decisions.

The types also can be put in one of three dominant emotions: Anger, Fear, or Shame.
> Eight, Nine, One – Anger
> Two, Three, Four – Shame
> Five, Six, Seven – Fear

I have given you a lot of information on the Enneagram and there is actually much more than you can delve into. Use as much or as little as you like when building your characters. If you choose to use a lot, think of it as layers. You start with your basic One (for example) and then you can add their Subtype. After that, you can see how they would act under stress or security (keeping that same subtype). And (or) you can look at their Wing. All of this combined will give you options for how your character might act in a variety of circumstances.

Have fun with it.

Chapter Two:

Step by Step
(Build Your Own Character)

    The Enneagram is a great tool and I love to use it to get an overall picture of what a character might do. I also love it as a tool to think of plausible contradictions that a character could have or how that character might change when under pressure or feeling particularly relaxed. Honestly, it is the best thing I've found to truly understand a character and people.

    However, starting with the Nine Types is not going to give you the subtleties you need for your character and it won't direct you as easily to later steps in plotting like internal and external goal.

    So instead of eating that elephant whole. Let's go at it in bites.

    Or in this case, steps.

Nine Steps For Building Character

Step 1:

The first step when building your character is recognizing the **character's cloak or the mask**. I like to start here because it is the most obvious. This is how the world sees the character. This is the caring mom or the successful businesswoman. The carefree party girl or the devil-may-care playboy.

The character's cloak or mask is what, if they were real, you would think of them when you first meet them. It's how they present themselves to the world.

Step 2:

The second step is the **character's fear**. The character uses the mask to hide this. This is not a surface fear like Indiana Jones' fear of snakes. This is fear is subconscious. It's what drives a character to act how they do. It is probably the most important aspect of your character and his or her internal motivations.

Some examples of a character fear are fear of doing wrong morally, being betrayed, being weak emotionally or being seen as a failure. They are not fear of snakes, germs, etc. Those things can be used to represent the fear if you like, but there needs to be a deeper internal fear behind them.

(Look in the *Hello Plot Workbook* for a chart of possible fears and what type of mask that character might use to hide it.)

Step 3:

The third step in the Nine Steps of Building Characters is the character's **strength** which he uses as a **crutch** to cope with or cover his fear. This will be part of the mask. For a character who is afraid of being trapped, their mask might be that of a globe-trotting playboy. The strength this character might use as part of their mask and to hide this fear is their charm. They are the life of the party… not a care in the world, people love them. All good…

Step 4:

The fourth step is the character's **motto**. It is what the character tells himself to justify whatever it is he or she does to cover his or her fear. A motto is something a character might actually say in the book to another character or it might be said about them. I think it has more impact if the character says it, but they don't have. No one has to, but as the writer, it is good to have it in mind.

Examples of a motto could be "Second place is the first loser." or "Everyone lies." Both of these examples give the character a justification for their actions. "Second place is the first loser," justifies winning at all costs. "Everyone lies," (House M.D. in case you didn't recognize it) means that the character is justified in not trusting anyone… no matter how close they may be to the character.

Step 5:

The fifth step in the Nine Steps is a **characteristic the character admires in others**. This can be a sneak peek at who the character will become at the end of his journey–after his arc is completed (assuming you aren't writing a tragedy where the character chooses his fear over his true self). It's usually easy to pick a character that your character loves. Why? What does that person have or do that brings out that admiration?

Step 6:

The sixth step is the character's **weakness**. This is the characteristic that gets the character in the most trouble with his or her story's antagonist. Your character has to have a weakness. He or she probably has many, but this weakness helps drive the plot because it is the thing the character does that gets him or her into trouble. Your character isn't going to just be a victim of outside forces. No... he or she is going to cause some of his or her problems. He or she is going to be active, not just in fixing things, but in messing them up too.

Step 7:

The seventh step is the character's **dark side**. It is what the character could become at his worst. In some stories, like *A Christmas Carol* (which I detail in the next chapter) Scrooge starts the story in his dark side. In most genre novels today, however, the character doesn't arc quite as fully as Scrooge and the main character doesn't ever fully hit this place, or if he or she does, it isn't for long. That doesn't, though, mean they can't or shouldn't. And it is definitely something to have in your toolbox. Not just for your main character, but as a possible doppelganger antagonist too.

A doppelganger antagonist is an antagonist who matches your protagonist in many ways. They may share the same Enneagram type or past. It is a "but for the grace of God go I" antagonist. Your protagonist may fear this doppelganger just because he sees himself in him. He is the shadow self your protagonist fears becoming.

As Jung said, "People will do anything, no matter how absurd to avoid facing their own souls." With a doppelganger antagonist, you can force your protagonist to do this, literally on the page.

Step 8:

The Eighth step is the character's **core need**. This is what needs to be filled for the character to be his true and happy self. If this is filled, he won't need the mask any longer. The playboy needs to be okay with commitment. He needs to feel like he can settle down with one person in one place and still be interesting. Still be of value. The driven executive needs to come to terms with failure and realize that failure is okay. That failure doesn't make him unworthy or of less value.

Step 9:

And finally, the ninth step is the **true and happy self**. This is what the character would be like with his core need filled and his mask and fear abandoned. This is what we see in the end if your character fully arcs. The playboy is able to settle down and he's happy doing so. The driven executive risks failure does fail but walks away content. Their fear no longer has a hold on them and they can let go of pretenses. Sound the music, cue the tears of joy, and watch them ride off into the sunset.

That is (again) if you aren't writing a tragedy. If you are, your character sadly won't get here. The reader will be able to see what this true and happy self would have been, but he will also know your character failed in that journey, and hopefully, the reader will walk away with some message from this that is just as rewarding as the happy sunset in the alternative. Without the happy…

Chapter Three:
To All the Characters
I've Loved Before
(Character Examples)

Now that you've been introduced to the Nine Steps, I want to show you the Enneagram and the Nine Steps in action by breaking down characters you already know. As always, feel free to skip ahead. Also, this is my take on these characters. Being fictional, they can't actually take the test and tell us what they are. Someone else may have a different opinion.

Oliver Queen (Arrow) – One

Oliver Queen is a superhero, straight out of the comics. Queen is a somewhat typical superhero of the billionaire variety. In his previous life, he was a spoiled rich boy who partied and didn't consider anyone except himself. In the show, *Arrow*, we see this. We also see the big event that changed him, being in a shipwreck and stranded on an island and forced to learn and do things it had never occurred to him to learn or do.

This past self probably makes you think Queen is or was a seven. There is, however, no seven in him in his current life. Real people, however, don't change their basic type. So first, let's acknowledge that Queen isn't a real person. Let's also acknowledge that while we see flashbacks to who he was in the past, we don't get as full of a picture as he is in the present. (So the one may have been there too.) And finally, if you look back at the Under Stress or Security part of the Enneagram, you will see that when feeling secure, a One will shift to a Seven. So it is completely possible that Queen was always a One, but the bits and pieces we see from his past are moments when he was secure and presenting as a Seven.

Okay, with all of that out of the way, why is Oliver Queen a One? Ones want to be good and have integrity. They fear being corrupt or defective.

Queen tells us these things about himself in the first episode when he is speaking to his family's housekeeper. "I want to be the person you always told me I could be." This need to be better, to not be defective is what drives him.

Being a comic book superhero means he comes with certain things like a literal mask that other fictional characters don't have. In my opinion, saying his Oliver Queen persona is his "mask" is a copout though, so I'm not going to do that. Instead, I tried to look to see what he used as a mask in both personas.

The **mask** he puts on is one of someone who doesn't care, not about other people, not about issues, really not about anything. He is told this numerous times by his ex-girlfriend. He doesn't embrace the playboy thing as much as you would expect him too, but he also doesn't let people see "his secret" which is, in my opinion, more than his secret identity. It's that he does care. That he knows he messed up and he wants more than anything to fix those mess ups.

This mask carries over to his superhero persona where he is calm and dispassionate in the execution of his mission. He rarely shows real passion or anger. He is just carrying out the tasks that he has assigned himself.

I already touched on his **fear** somewhat, but more specifically than being defective, Queen believes he has failed people. He failed his father. He failed his ex-girlfriend. He failed her sister. And his father failed too. By not being the person Queen thought he was, he failed Queen. So while his fear is that he is defective, it is tied up in all of these past failures. He actually voices this fear early on to his ex-girlfriend. "I'm just going to hurt you again…"

The **strength/crutch** that he uses to keep his mask going, is the ability to stay calm and appear detached. My guess is this strength is one he used in his previous life as well. Being detached keeps people at a certain distance. It would make being the carefree playboy all that much easier to pull off.

A basic One motto is "Right makes might and I am right." Queen's **motto** is probably a variation of that he "need(s) to right the wrongs done by his family."

The **characteristic he admires in others** is shown in his interactions with his ex-girlfriend. She is obviously the person he cares about the most. He carries her picture with him throughout the island ordeal, even though he had just cheated on her with her sister (and caused that sister's death). This girlfriend is another One, "always trying to save the world." She doesn't fail people. She sticks with them, even when the odds are extremely slim that she will succeed. She is the opposite of how Queen, in his heart, sees himself.

Queen's **weakness** is typical for a One. He's rigid and expects others to live up to standards that he has now set for himself. This is shown a lot with his dealings with his sister and his mother. He expects his sister to not make the same mistakes he made, and he expects his mother to do a better job with his sister than he feels she did with him.

His **dark side** would be giving over to his cause completely and losing any ability to be flexible in seeing that people will at times fail and that that is okay.

His **core need** is to accept his past failures and be okay with his faults and past mistakes.

To be his **true and happy self**, Queen would need to be able to accept that his father wasn't perfect, and neither was Queen. He would have to be okay with both of those things. He could continue to fight the bad guys, but with more balance. They would be more than a name on a list. He would see the world more in shades of grey and less in black and white. He wouldn't feel he had to "right the wrongs done by his family." He might still want things to be better, but it would not be a driving need that guided everything else in his life.

Dr. James Wilson (House, M.D.)– Two

Dr. James Wilson from House, M.D. is the main character, Gregory House's, best friend and a fellow doctor at Princeton-Plainsboro Teaching Hospital. He is, as a character reminds House in a later season, House's "conscience." He is also, though, an enabler of House's bad behavior.

Why is he an enabler? Because as an Enneagram Two, Dr. Wilson needs to be needed. He is driven to help people and when this is paired with a personality like House's this "help" is often not all healthy for anyone. We see this most in the last two seasons as both characters are faced with serious challenges.

Wilson's **mask** is that of the responsible adult, especially when compared to his friend House. He is House's conscience and many times protector, usually without House asking for or even wanting his protection. He comes across as the "good guy" who does the right thing. However, as the series goes on we discover many things Wilson has done that aren't "right" although he works hard to justify these acts in his own mind.

Wilson has a history of failed relationships. He also has a brother with schizophrenia who Wilson has lost touch with. His not 100% healthy relationship with House is perhaps his longest lasting and most important to him.

Wilson wants to be liked, by everyone. This makes him give into other's wishes and even not always give patients the advice they need to hear. It also makes him put himself and his career at risk when faced with an option of self-preservation or helping someone else. But the "help" isn't always the best help…it's the help that will make the other person happy, or that somehow Wilson thinks will make them happy. In reality, even though his patients and most people love him, this help drives some away.

His **fear** is that he will offend someone or not be liked. His **strength/crutch** that he uses to hide this fear is his nice guy persona and willingness to do anything to help another person.

Wilson doesn't speak his motto as succinctly as many characters do, but it is said about him by another character, "…Enduring pain to do some good for someone you care about. Isn't that what life is?"

House and Wilson are both the perfect match for each other and also the worst match. Wilson enables House, and House mocks him for it. Wilson cares so much that he is valued by others, that he is needed, and House doesn't care at all about either of those things. House doesn't need strokes or reinforcement from any outside force. In fact, he rejects those accolades. Wilson, however, needs to be needed. House's independence from this is the **characteristic that** both annoys Wilson about House and that **he admires**.

Wilson's **weakness** is also his strength. He is too willing to do anything to help others. He will put himself at risk and he will enable poor choices of others. He can't pull himself back enough emotionally to not help, even when he has to know that help will be detrimental to himself or others.

We see Wilson's **dark side** as he plummets under his diagnosis of cancer. House is not Wilson. Even though House definitely loves Wilson, probably more than he has loved anyone, House can't or won't express it in a way that Wilson needs. Wilson degenerates in a two-like manner, blaming others for not reciprocating for all the love and help he has given them. He expects them to be him, but that just isn't how people, especially House, work.

Wilson, "I'm pissed because I'm dying, and it's not fair. And I need... I need a friend. I need to know that you're there. I need... I need you to tell me that my life... was worthwhile, and I... I need you to tell me that you love me."

House replies, "No. I'm not gonna tell you that unless you fight."

Wilson's **core need** is to feel secure with himself and not need reinforcement from others.

Wilson' **true and happy self** would be a bit of a mix of who he is and his friend House. He needs to be secure enough to risk making people not like him, to let people make their mistakes and live with the consequences. He needs to realize the world doesn't need him fixing everything for it.

Scarlett O'Hara (Gone With The Wind) — Self-Preservation Three

Scarlett O'Hara is one of my all-time favorite characters. She grows and changes and UNgrows throughout the book and movie. We see her good and bad. We root for her and yell at her. She has complications and surprises, but throughout all of this, she still manages to be a 100% believable character.

When we first meet Scarlett, we can't miss her **mask**. She's the Southern belle to challenge all Southern belles. She's coquettish and fun and has all the men wrapped around her finger. She's beautiful and delicate. Much too much of a lady to spend time thinking about, well much of anything, or getting a single perfect finger dirty.

"Fiddle-dee-dee." Scarlett has her mask down cold.

And then war breaks out and Scarlett's world is upended. Being the Scarlett she portrayed to the world no longer brings Scarlett the rewards it once did because those rewards no longer exist.

Scarlett has to change and change she does. (Although she doesn't completely forget or lose the mask… she just has a lot less opportunity to don it for her benefit.)

Scarlett's **fear** is that she is worthless, or in Scarlett's case not the person at the tip top of worth. In the beginning of the story, this comes out in her search for the perfect husband. Later it appears as she tries to maintain appearances even when visiting Rhett in jail.

Scarlett's **strength or crutch** that she uses to cover her fear and maintain her mask is her beauty and stature in the Southern society. After the war starts, she loses both to a degree. Her stature is meaningless, and the need to work to survive robs her of what she sees as important aspects of her beauty.

Scarlett's **motto** is "I'll think about that tomorrow." This motto justifies not dealing with the hard stuff, especially the emotionally hard stuff. Instead, she can plow ahead in her three-way concentrating on the task at hand.

Scarlett doesn't admire a great many people. In fact, she holds most people and even the grand cause of the South in a bit of disdain. She does though **admire** her father Gerald O'Hara tremendously. Why? He's described as "vital and earthy and coarse." Nothing that a Southern Belle like Scarlett should admire, but she does. Her father has the freedom that as a Southern woman, Scarlett doesn't have. He can be who he is and still be held in regard. He doesn't have to don the careful mask she feels she does to be accepted and revered. She also admires strength. Later in the book, we see this when Melanie helps her dispose of the body of a dead Yankee who Scarlett has killed. Scarlett sees behind her "dovelike eyes" a "thin flashing blade of unbreakable steel." Melanie, it turns out, is more than Scarlett had credited her with being.

Scarlett's **weakness** that gets her into trouble is her vanity. It pops up over and over in the book. She has to dress up to see Rhett in prison, she declares she will never have another child because of the toll carrying one takes on her waistline. Scarlett just can't give up her need to be the prettiest girl at the top of the social ladder.

Scarlett's **dark side** is shown in her obsession with Ashley. For her, he represents status and class. Everything she thinks is important in her world and to her, and she would be willing to do anything to get him. Even lose everyone who truly cares about her. Ashley and Tara and what they represent are all that matters. She is driven and mean to others. She is self-centered and focused on her goal at all costs to others.

And cost her it does.

Scarlett's **core need** is to feel valued for herself. To realize that appearances are not important. To relax and enjoy simpler things. We see peeks of this happening, but tragedy strikes and Scarlett is sent spinning back to her old ways.

Scarlett's **true and happy self** would be one where she didn't care about appearances. Where she wasn't worried about her worth. She would be able to love Rhett and be loved. She would let go of what Ashley represented to her and value what Rhett and others offer. And maybe she does… just maybe she will get that all worked out tomorrow…

Jughead Jones (Riverdale) – Four

Jughead Jones in *Riverdale* is not the Jughead you remember from the Archie Comics. There are definite nods to the original, like a toned-down version of Jughead's iconic hat, but without those nods and the name, I doubt you would put the two together.

This Jughead is an introspective loner. He's an onlooker who hasn't really figured out his place in the world yet. He's part of the inner "cool kids" circle, but would never call himself one of them.

His **mask** is that of an aloof outsider, someone who doesn't care about fitting in. He is actually very free in telling us this. "I'm the damaged, loner outsider from the wrong side of tracks."

His **fear,** that he's not worthy of love, can be tied directly to his rough beginnings: a mother who abandoned him and a drunken father who's part of the local gang.

The **strength/crutch** that he uses to maintain his mask is his intelligence. Jughead is smart. He can figure things out that others can't, and he can write. Both of these abilities play majorly into the plot of the series. Jughead is a part of the brainpower behind solving mysteries, and his goal to write about the town of Riverdale is the premise for the actual telling of its story/the series itself.

His **motto** is "I'm weird… I'm a weirdo." He reinforces this view of himself frequently, and it gives him permission for not fitting in. It also helps cover his fear. If he is a weirdo, then it isn't necessarily that he isn't worthy of love, it's just that others won't get him. And if they *won't* get him… why put himself out there to see?

The **characteristic admires in others** comes from Betty. Yes, that Betty… the blonde cheerleader who in the comics has little more than sweetness and her looks going for her. However, like Jughead, the Betty in *Riverdale* is much different. As an Enneagram One, Betty has conviction. Maybe sometimes blind conviction, but she has it. And she's brave. She puts herself in uncomfortable positions for her cause without blinking an eye.

His **weakness** is the insecurity that makes him doubt his actions, where Betty will plow forward. Jughead is smart and good-looking and loved by those close to him, but he somehow still can't claim the confidence that all of that should give him.

Jughead's **dark side** always feels close. He could easily become the kid who withdraws completely. He could easily become completely self-destructive.

His **core need** is to accept that he is worthy of love, to see that people do love him, a lot, and quit looking for whatever other affirmation he seems to constantly be in search of.

We see some moments of Jughead in his **true and happy self**: confident, excited about the project at hand, and hopeful for his future. But then, something goes wrong and he crumbles, waiting to be built up again.

Scrooge (A Christmas Carol) – Self-preservation Five

There are few characters more associated with Christmas than Ebenezer Scrooge. You have to wonder if when Charles Dickens created the penny-pinching misanthrope, he had any idea of the longevity Scrooge would enjoy, or that of all of Dickens' novels *A Christmas Carol* would be the one most well-known....and who can we thank for that?

Scrooge.

What is it that makes Scrooge a character with such longevity? Let's break him down a bit, but first a description of him in Dickens' own words.

"...he was a tight-fisted hand at the grindstone, Scrooge! A squeezing, wrenching, grasping, scraping, clutching, covetous old sinner! Hard and sharp as flint, from which no steel had ever struck out generous fire, secret, and self-contained, and solitary as an oyster."

Sounds lovely, doesn't he? This low start, of course, makes Scrooge's transformation all the more rewarding. He arcs and that, in a nutshell, is what makes him great. Watching Scrooge change from this very harsh beginning into someone who appreciates the people around him, and not just his money, is rewarding. We don't read and re-read *A Christmas Carol* because we like the plot. It is, after all, a tad basic. We read and reread, and film and refilm, Scrooge's story because we want to watch Scrooge change.

Now for the breaking down part...

Scrooge's **cloak or the mask** is that he is cheap and mean. Everyone in the town knows it, but Dickens also lets us see that despite Scrooge's harsh treatment of his clerk, Bob Cratchit, Cratchit doesn't hate his boss. In fact, Cratchit defends Scrooge to his wife. This lets us know that there is hope for Scrooge. Cratchit is capable of seeing behind the mask that Scrooge has so carefully constructed. Scrooge wants people to believe his mask is real because it keeps people from getting close to him. But Cratchit isn't fooled.

Your average reader if asked what Scrooge's **fear** is at the beginning of the book would probably say he fears losing his money–he is a miser. But even if this were true, it isn't deep enough. Scrooge's obsession with money isn't his real issue. He just uses it to hide his real fear from others and himself.

So what is Scrooge's fear? Flip to the end of the story. What does the Ghost of Christmas Yet To Come show Scrooge that fills him with enough horror that he changes his ways? Does he lose his money...well, yes, but only after he is dead. So he had his money right up to the end.

No, what the Ghost of Christmas Yet To Come shows Scrooge is Scrooge dying alone, unmourned, and unimportant to anyone except the Cratchits who he has in many ways treated the worst. He has his money and his possessions, but he has nothing else. He has no one.

So what is his fear? A little back story goes a long way to pinning down a character's fear and Dickens gives us that with the first ghost, the Ghost of Christmas Past. "At one of these a lonely boy was reading near a feeble fire; and Scrooge sat down upon a form, and wept to see his poor forgotten self as he used to be." Then the Ghost of Christmas Past takes us to Scrooge at school. "...that there he was, alone again, when all the other boys had gone home for the jolly holidays. He was not reading now, but walking up and down despairingly."

The ghost even gives us a glimpse at a time when Scrooge was happy, first when his sister comes to school to get him and later when he is an apprentice in a job similar to what he does now. Was he surrounded by money? No, he was poor, but he was accepted and surrounded by people. He at that point belonged.

What the ghost doesn't show us is what happened between this happy time and the next scene where Scrooge's fiancé leaves him because he loves his money more than her. This is a bit of a gap, but we know from other parts of the book that somewhere in here Scrooge's sister, the one person with whom he had a true relationship, dies while giving birth to her son, Scrooge's nephew.

So in my mind, Scrooge's fear is of being alone and perhaps more specifically abandoned. He was abandoned as a child when his mother died during his birth. He was subsequently abandoned emotionally by his father who blamed Scrooge for his wife's death. He was abandoned by his sister Fan when she died, and he was abandoned by his fiancé. (Even though Scrooge's own actions pushed the fiancé away, he was still abandoned. Her actions just confirmed his fear even more.)

Scrooge's **strength** or **crutch** is his ability to amass wealth. Focusing on this keeps him from feeling the bite of being alone. He also believes that he can, by hoarding, keep at least his money from abandoning him.

Scrooge's **motto** is "money matters." If money matters then he doesn't have to spend time on other things, like people.

The fifth step is a **characteristic the character admires in others**. Who did Scrooge admire? His sister who Dickens describes as "brimful of glee." She is open and loving and filled with hope for a father who had emotionally abandoned Scrooge at his birth.

The sixth step is the character's **weakness**. Scrooge is full of weakness, but the one that gets him in trouble with the antagonist (who is Scrooge himself), is his lack of empathy. Until he can feel empathy for others, others won't feel empathy for him, and he will remain alone.

Scrooge's **dark side** is where we start the story. He is his dark side. *A Christmas Carol* is a story of redemption, a fine and somewhat common theme for Christmas stories. (*The Grinch* and *It's a Wonderful Life* are two other examples.) In most genre novels today, however, the character doesn't arc quite as fully as Scrooge.

Scrooge's **core need** is to feel the love and acceptance he felt with his sister, but more than that, he needs to realize that if someone leaves, he will still be okay.

And finally, the ninth step is that **true and happy self**. What the character would be like with his core need filled and his mask and fear abandoned.

Dickens shows us this too. He gave us a peek early on with the flashback to the young Scrooge being greeted by his sister, but in the end, Scrooge is completely transformed. He chuckles and buys turkeys.

He even goes to see the nephew he has avoided. He has more than completed his arc. And that, from a modern perspective, would be my only issue with the tale. Scrooge's transformation is a bit over the top and probably not completely fitting with the character Dickens drew from the start.

But then it is Christmas... a time for miracles.

Dr. John H. Watson (Sherlock) – Six

In fiction, you see certain types in certain roles quite often. You also see certain pairings quite often. This is the case with the Enneagram Five and the Enneagram Six. The *thinker* and the *skeptic* make a great match for detective type fiction. And there is no more classic detective fiction or pair than Sherlock Holmes (a five) and Dr. Watson (a six).

In the TV series *Sherlock*, Dr. John Watson is again a six. In this case, he earns the Six tag *loyalist* most obviously. In fact, his loyalty to Sherlock is so quick and so complete that it is commented on by more than one character in the first episode.

Watson is an army doctor, freshly returned from Afghanistan. He's having a rough time adjusting to life after war and is seeing a psychiatrist to help him through. He presents with a limp and hands that shake. The psychiatrist has told him that the limp is psychosomatic and that his shaking hands are due to PTSD. According to Sherlock, she is right on the first one. According to Sherlock's brother, she is wrong on the second.

Both brothers (in separate scenes) agree though that what Watson needs, what will cure both his shaking hands and his limp, is a return to danger. He wasn't traumatized by the war as you might think. He is lost without the constant threat and danger.

Life with Sherlock brings those back to him and almost immediately both the limp and the shaking hands are in his past.

By the middle of the first episode, their friendship is cemented, and Watson is 200% loyal to Sherlock who he has known only a few days.

On meeting Dr. Watson, you would not (if you were a normal person and not one of the Holmes brothers) suspect that he was a danger and an adrenaline junkie. He's calm and tends to stay at the back of the room as Sherlock engages with dead bodies, annoyed police, and others. Watson may have the same appetite for excitement as Sherlock, but he is not labeled by others as a psychopath or sociopath or any of the other less than positive tags Sherlock earns. Watson not only blends, he appears to be a completely upstanding citizen. And he is. He just enjoys his citizenry with a bit more death and mayhem than the average chap. He wears the **mask** of a calm, dependable person.

Watson is a good soldier. This is also commented on in the show. As a good soldier, he looks for dependable guidance. Once Sherlock has proven himself to Watson, Sherlock provides this. A typical **fear** for a Six is being without guidance. This fits Watson, but I'd take it a bit further and say he fears not having purpose and direction. When his wartime was over before he found Sherlock, he was lost, and his psychosomatic health issues appeared.

Watson's **strength and the crutch** that he uses to maintain his mask is his reliability. You can depend on Watson. He will be there when you need him. He won't let you down.

Sixes are wily creatures, the hardest of the Nine Types to nail down and identify completely. Maybe because of that, I had a hard time coming up with a **motto** for Watson that he actually says in the show. If I were to write one myself for him it would be "Go down with the ship." This is a typical Six motto, loyal to the end, and it definitely fits Watson. An example of this is at the end of the first episode when Watson has killed a serial killer when he was no personal threat to Watson and wasn't for certain to Sherlock either. Still, Watson shot the man and seemed completely unfazed by the act. Sherlock points this out, "You have just killed a man." Watson replies, "Yes, that is true, isn't it? But he wasn't a very nice man."

Given the choice of protecting Sherlock and killing someone, Watson has no qualms about the choice he made.

So far as the **characteristic Watson admires in others**, he reveals this later in the series, when he believes Sherlock is dead. Standing over his grave, he clearly says, "You were the best man, the most human... human being that I've ever known, and no one will ever convince me that you told me a lie, so... there. I was so alone... and I owe you so much."

Sherlock speaks the truth no matter how hard the truth may be for others to hear. This is the kind of trait that can cause problems in many relationships, but it is what Watson values most.

Watson's **weakness** is commented on a number of times in the series. He is addicted to dangerous people. Even his wife who presents herself as a completely normal upstanding citizen turns out to have a hidden dark side. When presented with this revelation, Watson asks Sherlock if everyone he had ever met was a psychopath. Sherlock in true form doesn't hold back the truth. "John, you're addicted to a certain lifestyle! You're abnormally attracted to dangerous situations and people, so is it truly such a surprise that the woman you've fallen in love with conforms to that pattern?"

Watson's **dark side** is revealed to us to a degree in the beginning when he has lost his purpose. To compensate, his mind creates fake ailments. If he'd been left without purpose and no one he trusted, this could have gone even further. He could have become reclusive or even destructive to others. He would have sunk into a pit of self-pity and skepticism, not letting anyone pull him out of it and back into the world.

Watson' **core need** is to trust himself. In the series, Sherlock fills this need, but trusting in Sherlock is not the same as trusting in himself. It's more of a bandage than a cure.

If Dr. John Watson were to find his **true and happy self**, he would let go of his fear of being without guidance and trust himself. He would also find purpose in something other than the most dangerous of situations. He would continue his friendship with Sherlock, but he wouldn't need it to maintain his healthy six status.

Lucifer Morningstar (Lucifer)– One-to-One Seven

Lucifer, from the TV show *Lucifer* (also from *DC Comics*, but I'm using the TV show for my reference), is a fabulous Seven, full of performance and enthusiasm and reckless acts of self-destruction. I'm using the term One-to-One for his subtype, but if you have watched the show, you know the other name for this subtype, sexual, fits him like a demonic glove.

Lucifer's **mask** is obvious. He's Lucifer, the devil. He cares about nothing and no one. He's a monster… a carefree and fabulous monster. And fun… oh, so much fun. It's all he cares about.

Or is it?

When we first meet Lucifer, he's being pulled over by a cop for speeding. Using his devilish charm (and supernatural power) he gets the police officer to admit that he too breaks the law by sometimes turning on his siren and speeding, just because he can.

Lucifer's response? "Why wouldn't you? It's fun!"

Later though when the starlet he'd helped is gunned down, we see quite clearly that Lucifer cares about much more than just fun. He finds the man who killed her, who is almost dead himself, and brings the man back to life enough to force him to tell Lucifer why he shot her. Lucifer returns to the girl's body and with Lucifer standing there, looking down at her, we see he isn't his mask. He cares about others, especially those who have been wronged, deeply. (Although he will claim, it isn't caring. It's simply that some people "are far too interesting" to let die.)

We see Lucifer's **fear** in the episode too. Speaking to his brother, the perfect angel, the one "dear old dad" loved best, he asks, "Do you think I'm the devil…"

Lucifer *is* the devil. He never hides this, but his fear is that he isn't just the devil in name, but that he is actually the devil in spirit too. If I were to put his fear into a general type, I'd call it "fear of being unworthy." Or in Lucifer's case, perhaps "worthy," but of something negative, of being made the devil by his father. Is he truly somehow morally corrupt? Is he a bad person? All of these are variations of his fear.

So far as **strengths**, Lucifer has many. He's the devil; he's charming and entertaining. People are drawn to him. He is also a supernatural being with the power to get people to tell him "what they truly want" and can't be killed by a normal human (in most circumstances). He uses his more human strengths as a **crutch** much more than he does his supernatural ones. Why? Because those strengths are part of his mask, what he uses to protect himself from his fear and anyone getting close enough to him for him to have to face that fear.

Lucifer's **motto** is that "Someone out there needs to be punished." In his mind, he isn't trying to prove anything. He doesn't even have *good* intentions (according to him). No, those who do bad just have to be punished, and he is here to do it. He is "a responsible devil." But he "just like(s) to play in general."

Lucifer would deny that he admires anything other than the most shallow of things in other people. He happily declares admiration for people's looks and craftiness, but these things aren't the characteristics he really admires. The **characteristic he admires in others** is security, their ability to put down their guards and love and be loved while trusting that they can still be themselves.

Lucifer's **weakness,** what gets him into trouble, is in a great deal his mask. Playing a carefree devil who only looks for fun is what gets him into hot water with the people most important to him. And when people get too close, when things get too real and he might have to face his fear, he acts out by drinking and having sex and playing as only a devil can play. His weakness is also his strength. He's fun and can bring others fun as well.

Lucifer's **dark side** is obvious. He's the devil, and yes, he slips at times into true devil mode, devil eyes/face, etc. But it's more complicated than that. What causes Lucifer to slip is giving up the hope that he is something other than what his father labeled him. He only truly becomes the devil, when he thinks he is nothing more than the devil. When he gives into his fear.

What all this adds up to is a devil with the **core need** of accepting who he is and trusting that he's okay. That he is worthy of being loved.

If Lucifer were to become his **true and happy self,** he wouldn't have to tell people he was the devil all the time. He wouldn't have to claim people were just interesting or that some people needed to be punished. He'd accept that he actually cares about others, and he wouldn't keep people at (dark angel) wing's length to keep from having to deal with the reality that he does actually care... and care deeply.

He would be secure and happy, devil and human. He would be imperfect, but whole and know that's okay. And he wouldn't care if his father thought he was worthy or not.

Eduardo Bernal (Shut Eye) – Eight

Eduardo Bernal is a bit of a stereotype for an Enneagram Eight. He's a mob boss. A lot of mob bosses in fiction are Eights. Probably a lot in real life too, but I don't personally know any to profile…

Back to Eduardo…

When we first encounter Eduardo, he's meeting with the main character, Charlie, who is a "psychic." Eduardo is telling Charlie that Eduardo's son has been diagnosed with Asperger's, and Eduardo wants Charlie to "fix" him.

Like Oliver Queen, as a mob boss, Eduardo has a bit of a literal mask. He's living as a law-abiding citizen and presents himself as such to Charlie, even though Charlie and his wife suspect he isn't.

The important part of Eduardo's **mask** is that he's calm and caring. He's a loving father who wants the best for his family.

We also, though, in this first meeting get a hint at what Eduardo **fears**. He makes it clear that he trusts Charlie and that that trust is both important to him and doesn't come easy. Eduardo fears betrayal.

To maintain his **mask** Eduardo has to maintain an image of calm. His strength is the ability to maintain that calm even under extreme situations. We see this in the first episode as well when a car drives by and shoots at Charlie's house while Eduardo is having a reading. Eduardo pulls out a gun but doesn't lose his cool. Before he leaves, Charlie shares a vision he'd had about Eduardo's son… revealing that the boy doesn't have Asperger's at all, but instead has a hearing issue that is curable. As Eduardo leaves, he says, "I won't forget this. Any of this." Like many Eights, Eduardo loves justice or his idea of what justice is. He'll work to see it done.

In the next episode, we see another aspect of Eduardo's personality. Charlie's diagnosis was right. Eduardo's son had a cyst in his ear and is now cured. This secure, happy Eduardo moves from his natural Eight into an Enneagram Two and takes care of Charlie and his wife by having a "crew" come and fix the damage done by the shooting.

After this, Charlie goes with Eduardo to meet some people that Eduardo is worried about. Charlie tells him he's in need of some assistance. Eduardo responds with a typical **motto** for an Eight, "Top of the food chain. Only place to be."

This combined with his not forgetting anything, good or bad, and another statement he'd made earlier that "Fools can be dangerous." tells us a lot about Eduardo and his outlook on life. He wants to be on top. It's the only place to be, and he is very aware of people who might want to take him down or help him stay there.

This suspicion combined with loyalty is actually very six-like, but this is more a natural offshoot of living the life Eduardo does, than an actual shift in personality type. Overall, he's a natural leader with a can-do attitude who as we see in the next scene can be completely ruthless when threatened.

Eduardo and Charlie enter a donut shop where Eduardo confronts a young man who Eduardo suspects has betrayed him. Eduardo maintains his mask of calm demeanor. So much so that Charlie doesn't hesitate to tell him that the man is lying. Still calm, Eduardo shoves the man into a vat of bubbling hot oil and holds him in until he is dead. Afterward, he picks a donut up off the floor and eats it.

Still calm.

We see the **characteristic Eduardo admires in others** when he feels Charlie has let him down. He arrives at Charlie's house to help Charlie dispose of a dead body. As Charlie is discussing how they are going to move the body, he interrupts him. "Hey, didn't I show you loyalty? Right here in this house. I credit you with miracles and you shit on our friendship." Turns out, even after one man was killed for betraying Eduardo, two more followed through. Eduardo blames Charlie and tells him he is either a "…liar or a fraud." Eduardo's previously high opinion of Charlie is lost, and Charlie has to talk his way out of

Eduardo's anger. (Incidentally, one of the few times we see Eduardo's mask slip and he allows his anger to be visible to others.) He had thought Charlie was real… trustworthy and now he doesn't.

Eduardo's **weakness** appears when his fear is activated. He's intolerant and hot-headed. This is at odds with his mask of calm which he maintains very well, but his anger is intense, and his actions can be extreme as we see when he pushes the man into the donut oil.

As a mob boss, you might argue that Eduardo is already living his dark side, but honestly, he has things under control most of the time. He is able to keep his weakness under control and use his strength to maintain his mask. His true **dark side** would appear if he lost this ability. If he let his fear of betrayal send him into a spiral of anger and revenge, trusting no one and trying to destroy them all.

At his **core**, Eduardo needs security. He needs to not see every slight as a betrayal, to be able to cut people out of his life without it affecting him as much as it does.

If he were to attain his **true and happy self,** he wouldn't need someone like Charlie to tell him if someone was betraying him. He would be secure enough to have normal conversations with others and deal with any slight in a constructive manner.

That, though, is not Eduardo's path and honestly, as viewers, we have no desire to see that side of him. My guess is we wouldn't believe it if we did.

Steve Trevor (Wonder Woman) – Nine, One-wing

Steve Trevor is a spy whose plane is shot down during WWI. It lands within the realm of protection of Themyscira, the island home of the Amazons. Diana (Wonder Woman) swims out to save him and brings him to shore. Unfortunately, Steve is not alone. He was being pursued by the Germans who make it through Themyscira's protective fog. The Amazons, however, are already on the scene and an epic battle ensues. Steve joins the Amazons in the fight and they prevail, but sadly, the Amazons lose a number of their members to the Germans' guns.

Steve is taken prisoner and forced to tell who he is, what he is doing on their island, and what is happening in the world.

When Diana learns of the war, she knows she is meant to end it. She frees Steve, and they take off together to London.

Nines want peace and harmony and are not the type to dive into a fight, so it may seem strange that I'm typing Steve, a full-fledge spy, active in the fight against the Germans, as a Nine. However, he reveals early on how this came to be. "My father told me once, he said, 'If you see something wrong happening in the world, you can either do nothing, or you can do something.' And I already tried nothing."

Nines are conflict-adverse, but that doesn't mean they won't join a fight if they feel they have to. Steve tried staying out of the fight. That didn't work.

Even then, the job he chose for himself is one where he is told to observe and report. It's the perfect job for a Nine who wants to do good. However, Steve's One-wing doesn't allow him to completely follow these orders and when he sees an immediate danger and an opportunity to stop it, he jumps on it. This act is what lands him in Themyscira.

You see other indications of his Nineness when they reach "no man's land." Diana a 2/1 (or 1/2… discuss amongst yourselves) wants to save the people suffering there. And while Steve is completely sympathetic to their plight and Diana's desire to help, he has focused on the bigger battle and wants them to move past this smaller one. She says, "So we do nothing?" He replies, "No, we are doing something! We are! We just… we can't save everyone in this war. This is not what we came here to do."

Nines avoid what upsets them and the situation at "no man's land" is very upsetting. Steve has committed to doing something, but he has chosen the less personal bigger fight and since the battle at this particular place has been going on for an extended time, there is no "now or never" threat to kick Steve out of Nine and into One. That is until Diana strides across the battlefield, gaining ground, and showing this cause is not lost. Then Steve rallies the others and plunges in too, going with his gut, which Nines are prone to do.

Steve's **mask** is of a man who is solid, but with a sense of humor. He doesn't show fear, although while trying to convince Diana of his honesty, he wraps the golden lasso around his wrist and speaks it freely, "We're probably going to die. This is a terrible idea!" He's calm, rational, and under control.

A typical Nine **fear** is of loss and separation. For Steve, I think it is more a fear that nothing matters. That he doesn't matter. In the context of this story, it's that he is there doing what he is supposed to do, but in the end, it will make no difference. "Maybe people aren't always good, Ares or no Ares. Maybe it's just who they are."

Steve's **strength** is his ability to withdraw emotionally. He can and does put distance between himself and the suffering. This allows him to keep his mask, both as a rational spy and actually when being a spy.

In *Wonder Woman*, we encounter Steve when he has already arced to some degree. He's already let go of his Nine desire to stay completely out of conflict. Because of this, we don't see the motto that he would have employed to justify that inaction. Instead, we see him as he struggles with deciding if Diana is right and humanity is worth saving. If he was right to engage. If he should, in fact, engage even more whole-heartedly. If he can make a difference. His motto here is simply, "We can't save everyone." My guess is that that was his motto before and he used it to justify staying completely out of the fight. Now, however, it is his justification for staying focused on the bigger fight and ignoring the smaller more personal atrocities that Diana is determined to rectify.

The **characteristic he admires most in others** is Diana's blind faith. She has no doubt that what she is doing is right. She has no doubt that every life matters, that the greater good does not outweigh helping individuals along the way. Then when she loses that faith, when she starts to question if humanity deserves saving, he argues back, "It's... it's not about deserve. Maybe, maybe we don't. But it's not about that, it's about what you believe. You don't think I get it, after what I've seen out there? You don't think I wish I could tell you that it was one bad guy to blame? It's not! We're all to blame!"

Steve's **weakness** is his indecision and lack of faith. He is in the fight, but he doubts if any of it will matter.

Steve's **dark side** would be giving up. Deciding that since he can't save everyone, he should save no one. He could dissociate from the world and retreat to a place where no one asked anything of him.

Steve's **core need** is to know that what he does matters. That even if his actions don't solve every problem, they still have value.

Steve does not have a typical happy ending in the movie. However, he does find his **true and happy self**. He gives up his doubt and accepts that doing what he can do is important, that he has a role to play in this world and it is valuable. He makes the hard choice because he "can save today." She "can save the world."

***

Now that we've gone through the types and examples of each, you are hopefully ready to take the Enneagram and build some great characters. Doing so will help you in the next step… plotting.

So, pick a character and fill out the following:

Form: Nines Steps for Your Character

Name:

Role:

Enneagram Type:

Wing?

Sub-type?

Mask:

Fear:

Strength/Crutch:

Motto:

Characteristic Admires Most in Others:

Weakness:

Dark Side:

Core Need:

True and Happy Self:

But before we move on completely from characters, I want to add one more level and give you a checklist for your most important characters.

Chapter Four:

You Ain't Character Enough to Lead This Story (Making Characters Great)

Starting with the Enneagram and working through the Nine Steps will certainly get you moving in the right direction with your characters and may even be enough, but if you want to give your characters an extra ratchet towards great, here are a few more things to consider.

What makes a book or movie special... makes it stick with you long after the cover is closed and the final credits have rolled? The special effects? The car chases? The slapstick comedy? Maybe for a while, but stories that really have lasting power contain one thing, great characters.

Scarlett O'Hara and Rhett Butler (*Gone with the Wind*), Rick Blaine (*Casablanca*), Atticus Finch (*To Kill a Mockingbird*), Jo March (*Little Women*) are just a few examples of characters that have proven to have staying power.

To see what I'm talking about, think about the big scenes for these characters, the scene where they came alive. For Scarlett it could be her standing out in that field, holding up that handful of dirt or her tearing down those curtains. Those scenes gave us a glimpse at a Scarlett we hadn't seen before–we'd seen hints that that strength was there, but not full evidence. And when those scenes revealed a truth about Scarlett we hadn't seen before, we loved her and she stuck with us.

The same is true for the others.

So how do you set these scenes up? How do you create characters that people will term *great*? Four simple things will get you well on your way...

• **Give them something to love and not just love but love deeply**. Give them something that they would sacrifice everything to save. Think of Scarlett with that handful of dirt. She had lost everything, every pretty dress, every party, her entire world, but she still had Tara. Tara was important to her.

• **Next, give them something that haunts them.** Ilsa stood Rick up at that train station in Paris. It destroyed him, destroyed the hopeful youth he had been. If this event hadn't happened in his past, if he hadn't still been carrying it around with him, Casablanca could not have been the story that it is.

• **Third, figure out what they think they can't or most don't want to do–then make them do it.** Rhett didn't want to join the fight; he didn't want to leave Scarlett. He did both and we loved him.

• **Along these same lines, have them contradict themselves or reader expectations of them.** Scarlett was a flighty "I'll think about it tomorrow" party girl, but she showed real grit when she had to. Rhett and Rick were disenchanted with life and tried to act as if they didn't/couldn't care about the cause of the day...but they did. They conquered their own pasts, fears, and weaknesses. Nothing makes a reader love a character more.

Do these four things, **show your characters doing them in scene**, and we will follow your characters anywhere.

Form: Make Your Characters Great

Name:

What this character loves and loves deeply...

What haunts this character...

What this character least wants to do or most doesn't want to do...

How this character contradicts himself (think mask versus reality)...

Part Two: Help Me Make It Through This Book

(The book you are writing that is…)

Chapter Five:

Let's Walk The Line
(Character and Plot)

Did you know there was a line between character and plot? A connection?

There is or should be. Your story is the intersection of character and plot. If you take a random character and drop him into a random plot, you will not have a story. For story, one must drive the other.

So how do we do that?

Easy.

Fear -> Core Need-> Internal Goal -> External Goal

If you did the Nine Steps for Building Characters for your main character, you already know the first two.

Let's say you have a character who fears she isn't worthy. This fear, as you know, is subconscious, but it leads to the character's core need of feeling she is worthy. This character doesn't walk around knowing she doesn't feel worthy or that she will only be happy if she gives up that fear, but it's there and she is always trying to fill that need/get rid of that fear. Those two things drive her through the story, which means they drive the plot.

Not Worthy-> Needs to Feel Worthy ->

What might your character do or work towards that would fill these things? What might make her think she was worthy?

What if this character was ignored by her mother? Would she maybe think (subconsciously) that if she could just get her mother's approval that everything else would be okay? That she would fill that hole in her world and be happy?

This is an example of what her Internal Goal might be. So...

Not Worthy -> Needs to Feel Worthy -> Wants Mother's Approval

A lot of writers get this far and then they stop. The problem with this is how are we supposed to know when she gets her mother's approval or doesn't? How many ways could she try to do this? Thousands? And how unfocused might that story wind up being?

For a strong plot and honestly, an easy to write story that *works*, we need a goal that is urgent, universal, important/personal, concrete.

Urgent means there's a deadline tied to it. It isn't enough that someone wants to save the world at some point in their life. They need to have to save it today! (Or whatever timeframe works for your story.)

Universal simply means it is something we all can understand. You don't want us to have to work to figure out what it is this character is trying to do. You want us to get it easily.

Important/personal means we need to believe that this goal is important to the character. I may not think winning a baking contest is important in my life, but as a reader, if I believe it is important to that character I will care about him/her entering it and the outcome.

Concrete means simply we can see it on the page, that we as readers will know if the character does or does not achieve the goal. Which means we need a physical representation of say getting her mother's approval.

So, what could a character's goal be that would achieve all
?

It is going to depend on your character's backstory, your interests, etc., but let's say our character is a theatre geek who has always gotten the understudy role. Her mother never comes to her plays because "Why bother?" She never brags about the character to her friends because "They won't have heard of you or that play."

But Broadway? If this character got a starring role in a Broadway play and not just any Broadway play, but one specific show with tryouts this week…?

Then, yes, we have a goal that is Urgent: She has to do it this week.

Universal: We know what a Broadway play is.

Important/personal: She's been acting all of her life.

Concrete: We will see her try out. We will see the callbacks. We will see her on stage or not.

And it all goes back to getting rid of that fear and filling that core need.

It is a plot driven by your character.

Not Worthy -> Needs to Feel Worthy -> Wants Mother's Approval-> Get Starring Role in Broadway Play (One particular one)

Now you have your characters and you have your character's goals, both internal and external. You may not yet appreciate how big of a deal this is, but it's huge. You are well on your way to plotting and writing your book.

Form: Character Story Goal

Name:

Fear:

Core Need:

Internal Goal:

External Goal:

   Urgent? How?

   Universal? How?

   Important/Personal? How:

   Concrete? How?

Chapter Six:
Almost Persuaded

In the last chapter, we worked out your character's internal and external goals, and you and I know that they are urgent, universal, important/personal, and concrete, but we also need to make sure the reader knows it.

What does that mean? Simple: motivation.

We need to know your character's motivation for having this goal.

Goal is what your character wants.
Motivation is why they want it.

Preferably what makes them want it *right now*.

In our Broadway play example, you and I know that she wants to get the lead role in a Broadway play to get her mother's approval, but why does she need to do this now? What event has happened in her life that triggered her to act on this now?

Maybe a friend got some great new job and her mother heard about it and was carrying on about how great the friend was? Maybe this happened at a party. Maybe at a party that was supposed to be about our character, but instead became about this friend?

All those maybes add up to not only motivation but also a scene, a scene that will explain why our character later dives headlong into the plot.

So, our character…

Wants: to get a starring role in one particular Broadway Play

Because: she wants to prove her mother wrong after she called our character out as a failure at her own birthday party (in scene)

Great we have a goal and we have a motivation. Are we ready to plot?

No. Not yet...

We need more. We need problems and not of the writing variety. Those will come... they always do.

No, we need problems for our character. She wants to get this starring role, but she can't just walk in and get it. That would be not only unlikely, it would also be boring.

We need **conflict**.

Conflict. Conflict. Conflict. Good fiction has to have it. Good fiction has to have lots of it. Yes, good fiction has to have conflict on **every page**.

But for now, let's just start with one over-arching conflict that is going to get in the way of our character reaching her major external goal.

She wants to star in a Broadway play. What could get in her way?

Maybe she can't sing. That would be a problem.

Maybe her best friend who she has sworn to help wants the role too.

Maybe her mother is trying to get her to give up acting and become a doctor.

The choices are infinite, but what you chose here should be the one big conflict that drives the plot.

Before you pick, I want you to think about one other thing.

Who or what do you want to be the major antagonist in this story? That person or thing should be the source of this major conflict.

So, let's take a step away from all of this and talk about antagonists.

Chapter Seven:
The Fightin' Side of Your Story
(Antagonist)

You've probably heard of the basic types of conflict you can have in literature: man-against-man, man-against-nature, man-against-self.

Most stories, however, have some kind of human (or something with human characteristics) as the antagonist and that is the type of conflict I'm going to address here.

So assuming you are working with some kind of man-against-man(ish) conflict, do you need an actual single human antagonist?

No, but... it is going to be a whole lot easier to write a moving story with a single human representation of the antagonist.

And by *single*, I don't mean that you can't have more than one antagonist in a book. You can. By *single* I mean if you are thinking of making your antagonist a group, you should also come up with a person to represent that group for one-to-one conflict.

In *Star Wars (Episode IV – A New Hope)* the antagonist is clearly Darth Vader. If there had been no Darth Vader and instead the conflict had been focused on the much bigger Galactic Empire, the story would have lacked focus. Viewers would not have been able to connect as strongly, and they just would not have cared as much. Darth Vader gave a personal face to the bigger conflict. That is important. That made us care.

Also consider that even if you are writing a man-against-self story, you should probably have some other human representation of that self for the character to face down one-on-one on the page. Think *Bridget Jones Diary*. Bridget was her own worst enemy. She was her own antagonist. However, Daniel Cleaver serves as a single human representation of all of her failings. Daniel gives us a way to see on the page/screen her battle which is much more entertaining and effective than her sitting in a room, drinking and talking to herself. (Which she does, but a full book of that would not have been entertaining.)

So, you need an antagonist, and from here on we are going to assume that antagonist is human(ish).

As I said in the Introduction, when I first started writing, I wrote a whole book with no antagonist. Okay, I actually wrote two whole books with no antagonists, but one of those was a mystery so I kind of snuck one in by default without realizing that was what I was doing.

The other was a romance and there was *NO* antagonist.

None.

It was horrible.

Really horrible.

I also though, to make things super fun, had no goal, no plot, and a whole lot of backstory, *but I digress...*

Let's for a minute talk about why I am putting antagonist here in pre-plot instead of character.

Simple, because your antagonist (even if human) is the most important element in driving your plot.

If you have no antagonist, you have no conflict.

If you have no conflict, you have no story.

Stuff happens, but stuff happening is not story.

Stuff happening is what that person you were stuck talking to at the cocktail party told you about his day. He went to the store. There was a long line. He bought shrimp. He drove home. He ate the shrimp. He fed his cats. He went to bed.

Stuff happened. And you are looking for a shrimp fork to stab in your forehead, so you will have an excuse to escape the telling of it.

What does his series of events need?

An antagonist.

Someone who stalks him through the store and follows him home, who he fights off with the help of his cats, and finally after a moment of complete fear and surety of failure, finds the courage and smarts to overcome with that shrimp fork to the forehead.

So… antagonist. Does your story have one?

Let's find out. Or find out if you have the right one. Ask yourself the following:

Form: Finding Your Antagonist

What is your protagonist's main external goal?

Who or what is keeping him from achieving this goal?

Is this one person? If a group, can you give it the face of one person? (Think Darth Vader, not the Galactic Empire)

What is your character's fear?

Who keeps them from over-coming this fear or enables this fear?

Can you put this person in a position where if they get what they want, the protagonists can't get what he wants?

How exactly do these two goals conflict?

In a romance, it's common to make the hero/heroine each other's antagonists. This keeps the main characters' goals tied to each other and forces them to interact in a way that strengthens the romance plot too.

If you aren't writing a romance, it is still best to have your protagonist and your antagonists in a position where they have goals that directly conflict with each other. If one gets what she wants, the other can't get what he wants.

This is the strongest conflict you can have... two directly opposing goals.

Two dogs.

One bone.

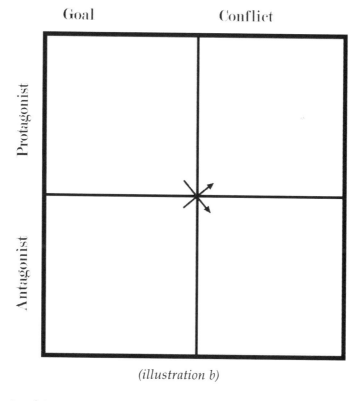

(illustration b)

So, in this case, we either need an antagonist with the same goal as our protagonist (Two Dogs One Bone) or we need an antagonist whose goal requires our protagonist to give up his goal.

In the case of our quest for the Broadway role, it would be that dream of getting that role.

The first is easy. There's another actress doing everything she can to get the role and our story will revolve around our protagonist's struggle against this person. The second gets more complicated but could be the better story to tell. Someone needs the protagonist to do something different and doing that something different sets up problems for the protagonist in practicing, making it to rehearsals, etc. This someone else could have completely altruistic intentions. They could even think they are helping our protagonist.

It could, for example, be a friend who believes our protagonist's true calling isn't acting at all, that her true calling is to help animals. This friend could have the goal of launching a pet rescue and needs our protagonist's help. Helping that friend is the conflict that gets in the way of our protagonist achieving her starring role. In our protagonist's subconscious mind it also gets in the way of gaining her mother's approval because there is no money or fame in rescuing dogs and her mother dedicated her life to taking our protagonist to dance classes and singing classes and everything she would ever need to be a star.

The friend's goal is starting this pet rescue (by a certain date or event, because it also needs to be urgent), but she needs her friends help and the friend is obsessed with this play.

So there you have two conflicting goals on which to build a plot with lots of conflict and movement to get you from start to end with no sagging middle.

Let's recap...

You have the Nine Steps for your protagonist. If you didn't do them yet for your antagonist or didn't know who your antagonist was going to be, now would be a good time to go back and do them for him too. In the case of the story we've been discussing, I would do them for the mother too, because she is going to most likely serve as a secondary antagonist.

You also know your protagonist's **Goal, Motivation, and Conflict**, also known as…

I want (goal):

Because (motivation):

But (conflict):

You also know these things for your antagonist, and ideally, the two fit nicely in the Goal/Conflict box (*illustration b*).

Want more help building your antagonist? Check out the Table of Contents for a link to the Bonus Material section of this book.

Now what?

Now we plot…

Part Three: You've Never Been This Far Before

Chapter Eight:

Tiger by the Tail
(Your Plot)

There are a lot of methods of plotting. I use a **12-step method**, which I outline in this chapter. Here you will find a description of each of these 12 steps and at times the Hero's Journey equivalent. (For more information on the **Hero's Journey** refer to the Bonus section of this book.)

I am giving you these 12 steps, but I don't suggest that you just plow through them in order. Instead, I suggest going on to Chapter Nine where I will lead you through what I find as a more organic method of plotting for most people. If that doesn't work for you, you can always return here and just plot each step in order.

Also, be aware that these steps may vary so far as order depending on the story you are telling. And while you will probably want to use all 12 points for your main story, you may also want to use at least some of these steps for each of your subplots. Meaning you may have an Inciting Incident, etc. for each subplot or character arc, in addition to one for the main plot. For a subplot to have some meat to it, I suggest hitting at least three of these plot points for it. (Most likely: Inciting Incident, Midpoint, and Climax)

1.) Ordinary World

The Ordinary World (also called this in Hero's Journey) is how your character's world looks before some big event happens that sets your character on a new path. In older fiction, this piece took up a much bigger part than it tends to in modern fiction. Depending on the type of fiction you are writing, your readers may have more or less love for Ordinary World. A lot of cozy mystery readers enjoy a nice chunk of ordinary world to get to know the characters, while thriller readers are more likely to want to be dropped right into the action. Know your readers when deciding how much Ordinary World to include and you may even decide not to include it at all.

The Ordinary World gives your readers a chance to connect with your characters before the action of the story gets going. This makes it popular with readers of more character-driven stories like women's fiction or cozy mysteries. It also allows you to set up a few rules of the world that you may want to draw on later. The Districts in *The Hunger Games* for example or the legends in *Moana*.

Another reason to include Ordinary World is to set up a comparison for the end of your story. If you let your reader see how things were before, it will make your character's arc more meaningful. It also allows you to do some fun things like "bookend" scenes where you put the character in a similar place or surrounded by the same people at the end of the book as we saw them in the beginning during their Ordinary World. This helps to really highlight how they have changed.

You also do not have to put the Ordinary World first. A lot of thriller type books move things either out of linear order or play with point of view in order to give their reader the bang by starting with the **Inciting Incident** (Step 2) while also offering some **Ordinary World** a bit later. A good example of doing this using both varying points of view and non-linear events can be found in *Mortal Prey* by John Sandford.

The protagonist of Sandford's Prey series is Lucas Davenport, a maverick detective. *Mortal Prey* is book 13 in the series, so the reader most likely already knows quite a bit about him, but Sandford still gives us a little look at Davenport's Ordinary World. He doesn't though lead with it. Instead, when the book starts, we see through the eyes of an omniscient narrator the victim of a shooting in a hospital bed. Then, still, with our omniscient narrator, we go back in time to see the whole event. This event is actually the **Inciting Incident** in *Mortal Prey*. It is the event that sets off all the other activity in the book. However, our hero, Davenport, isn't aware of it yet. So in Chapter 2, we meet Davenport in his Ordinary World and his point of view, checking out a house he is rebuilding.

Examples of Ordinary Worlds:

Bridget Jones Diary by Helen Fielding: Bridget on New Year's Day headed to her "mother's annual turkey curry buffet."

Moana: Moana growing up in her village where we learn the legend of Te Fiti and Maui and see that her father has a fear of going past the reef.

Mortal Prey by John Sandford: Lucas Davenport checking out his new house. (Chapter 2)

Star Wars: Episode IV - A New Hope: Luke at home taking care of the droids and having dinner with his aunt and uncle.

The Wonderful Wizard of Oz by L. Frank Baum: Dorothy at home. (In the book this is basically just a few paragraphs of description and backstory since once in scene they are waiting for the cyclone.)

2.) Inciting Incident

This is the event that kicks off the action in your story, that pushes your character to make some choice or embark on some journey that is the main purpose of your story. It is the event that kick-starts the rest of your story. For the Hero's Journey it corresponds with the "Call to Adventure," but you may have an Inciting Incident that is separate from the "call," such as I described in *Mortal Prey*. In that case, the attack we see at the beginning of the book is the Inciting Incident, but our main protagonist isn't there to see it. Thus his "call" comes later when he gets a literal call to investigate the case. You might even have an Inciting Incident that isn't seen on the page. An example of this might be an opening scene right after a bomb exploded. The Inciting Incident would have been the bomb, but we jump in the story right after that. (This would also be a story with no Ordinary World shown.)

In other stories, the Inciting Incident and the "Call to Adventure" may be one and the same. (If using Hero's Journey, you might also see a "Refusal of Call" where the character doesn't immediately take up the call in reaction to the Inciting Incident.)

There are even cases where you may choose not to show the Inciting Incident on the page. Dean Koontz does this in his Jane Hawk novel, *The Whispering Room*. Prior to the book beginning, Hawk's husband and a number of other people have committed suicide. We instead jump into the story with another soon-to-be apparent suicide. This is, in the overall story structure, more of a Raise the Stakes scene than Inciting Incident because Hawk was already on her path for this story.

Whether you decide to show the Ordinary World, start with the Inciting Incident, or skip them both, you still need to know what they are.

Examples of Inciting Incidents:

Bridget Jones Diary by Helen Fielding: Bridget overhears Mark Darcy insulting her.

Moana: A villager shows Moana that the coconuts are blighted, and the fishermen tell her all the fish are gone. (Moana attempts to "Accept the Call" here by trying to get past the reef in her canoe to find fish but fails.)

Star Wars: Episode IV - A New Hope: For the overall story, it's Princess Leia putting a message for Obi-Wan Kenobi and plans to the Death Star in R2-D2. For Luke, it is triggering the message on R2-D2 so he sees it.

The Wonderful Wizard of Oz by L. Frank Baum: Dorothy's house is picked up by the tornado. (In the movie, the Inciting Incident could instead be Toto being taken by Miss Gulch. You really need both the tornado and Miss Gulch to set things in motion in the movie.)

3.) Raise the Stakes

This is what happens after the Inciting Incident that makes it even more imperative that something has to be done. It ups the stakes of that Inciting Incident. What if Dorothy's house had just landed a mile away still in Kansas? What if it hadn't landed on the witch? By dropping the house in Oz and on the witch, Baum raised the stakes. That's what you want to do too.

Examples of Raising the Stakes:

Moana: Moana's father threatens to burn the boats which would destroy the heritage of her people. He is diverted by

Moana's grandmother's illness. This also though reinforces Moana's call and dream when the grandmother urges her to take the heart of Te Fiti and find Maui so he can return it.

Star Wars: Episode IV - A New Hope: R2-D2 runs away to find Obi-Wan Kenobi.

The Wonderful Wizard of Oz by L. Frank Baum: Dorothy's house lands in Oz on the Wicked Witch of the East.

4.) Protagonist Engages

Remember we don't want a protagonist who goes with the flow. We want an active protagonist. This point is here to remind you to do that. Something happened that raised the stakes for the protagonist. Now have your protagonist engage. Have her *do* something. This may be her "answering the call."

Examples of Protagonist Engages:

Moana: Unlike Luke in *Star Wars*, Moana is a very active protagonist. She "Accepts the Call" by taking one of the boats and then upon finding Maui, confronts him.

Star Wars: Episode IV - A New Hope: Luke is very slow to engage. As an Enneagram 9 is happy going with the flow. His first engagement is after he finds his home destroyed. He "Accepts the Call" from Obi-Wan. "I'm going to come with you to Alderaan." As a true 9, he required something big, like his home being destroyed, to push him into action. Even then we don't see him truly engaging/taking an active role in the fight (He doesn't even strike back in the bar brawl.) until the Millennium Falcon has been pulled into the Death Star and they realize Princess Leia is nearby. Then his 1 wing kicks in, and he convinces Han Solo to help him rescue her.

The Wonderful Wizard of Oz by L. Frank Baum: Dorothy puts on the witch's shoes and takes off down the yellow brick road.

5.) Antagonist Bites Back

We want an active protagonist, but we also don't want things to be too easy for him. As I said earlier, your antagonist is one of the most important elements of your story. This plot point is to make sure he is pulling his weight, that he is **actively** working *against* your protagonist. At this point, the battle is on.

Where is your antagonist? What is he doing? Specifically, what is he doing to get in the way of your protagonist reaching his goal?

Examples of Antagonist Bites Back:

Moana: At this point, Maui plays the role of antagonist. He steals Moana's boat and leaves alone. Soon after she overcomes this set back, they are attacked by the Kakamora, adding more conflicts and more opportunities for us to see Moana as the active protagonist she is.

Star Wars: Episode IV - A New Hope: The Death Star blows up Alderaan.

The Wonderful Wizard of Oz by L. Frank Baum: In the movie, Dorothy and her new friends are challenged by the Wicked Witch of the West and then a bit later encounter an enchanted poppy field created by her.

6.) Midpoint/Point of No Return

As the name indicates, this usually happens somewhere in the middle of your story. It's a turning point so big that it can feel like one story has ended and another is beginning. This is true in both *Star Wars* and *The Wizard of Oz*. In both one major goal has been completed and a new one presents itself. The protagonist is so deep in the fight now that there is no option for them to just turn back. They have changed too much. They need to see the battle/story out.

Examples of Midpoint/Point of No Return:

Moana: Moana and Maui retrieve his fish hook. This clears the way for Moana to return to her first goal, getting Maui to take the heart of Te Fiti back to the goddess.

Star Wars: Episode IV - A New Hope: Princess Leia is rescued and the group escapes to the Rebel base where they analyze the Death Star plans. (At this point Luke's goal changes to destroying the Death Star.)

The Wonderful Wizard of Oz by L. Frank Baum: Dorothy and her friends reach the Emerald City. (Note: Dorothy gets a new immediate goal here. In the book to kill the Wicked Witch of the West and in the movie to take her broomstick which most likely also means killing her.)

7.) Pinch/Tighten the Screws

After the protagonist commits to his new goal or is dealing with whatever major change has come his way at the Midpoint, something should happen to "tighten the screws" on him. Make things harder for him.

Examples of Pinch/Tighten the Screws:

Moana: Maui has his hook, but he can't shapeshift.

Star Wars: Episode IV - A New Hope: Han Solo leaves. With Han, Chewbacca, and Obi-Wan gone, Luke is now on his own.

The Wonderful Wizard of Oz by L. Frank Baum: (movie) The Wicked Witch of the West sends her winged monkeys after Dorothy and her friends. They are captured and brought to the Witch.

8.) Turning Point to Crisis

The protagonist makes a choice that leads to the crisis/the worst thing that can happen. The important thing at this step is to look back to your character work. What is your protagonist's weakness? What did you say would get him into trouble with the antagonist? Consider using that weakness here or using his strength. Either way, making the crisis of your protagonist's making increases pressure on him and makes the battle much more personal. It raises the stakes yet again.

Examples of Turning Point to Crisis:

Moana: Maui and Moana have arrived at the island of Te Fiti. Moana gives him the heart and he tries to get past Te Ka. She knocks him down. Moana, determined that she can do what he couldn't, tries to sail past Te Ka despite his objections. Maui uses his hook to ward off another attack by Te Ka and it is badly damaged. Angry, he tells Moana that he is nothing without his hook and that while "The ocean told you you're special and you believed it," "It chose wrong."

Star Wars: Episode IV - A New Hope: Luke draws on the Force, attracting Darth Vader's attention.

The Wonderful Wizard of Oz by L. Frank Baum: In the movie, Dorothy attempts to avert her Crisis by agreeing to give the Witch the ruby slippers, but the shoes won't come off.

9.) Crisis

The worst thing that can happen to your protagonist happens. This is where readers/viewers should think all is lost. There is no escape. No way to win. Write your character into an impossible to fix scenario and then figure out a way for them to fix it!

Examples of Crisis:

Moana: Maui leaves Moana alone on her boat. She has failed at her original goal which was to bring Maui to Te Fiti so he can return the heart.

Star Wars: Episode IV - A New Hope: R2-D2 is shot by Darth Vader. Luke is truly alone in the fight. (A brief Crisis, but still a Crisis.)

The Wonderful Wizard of Oz by L. Frank Baum: In the movie, Dorothy agrees to give the Wicked Witch her ruby slippers to save Toto but is unable to. She is locked in a tower with the hourglass of death, "ticking" down.

10.) Dark Moment

The worst has happened (Crisis) and all is lost. Here we see your character at their lowest emotional point. Let them visit this place, then kick them in the seat somehow and get renewed for the battle (Climax) ahead.

Examples of Dark Moment:

Moana: Having failed at her goal, Moana throws the heart back into the ocean. She is defeated, and we see it. "I'm not the right person."

Star Wars: Episode IV - A New Hope: Star Wars does not show a true Dark Moment for any of the characters. There is a fleeting one when all seems to be lost in the battle to destroy the Death Star, right before Han and Chewie return to help Luke.

The Wonderful Wizard of Oz by L. Frank Baum: Dorothy is trapped in the tower with the sand ticking down to her death. She breaks into tears and says, "I'm frightened. I'm frightened, Auntie Em. I'm frightened."

11.) Climax

Climax is THE scene! It's the one your reader/viewer has been waiting for. Your character was down and out in the Dark Moment. No way to win. But then... something happened that kicked him into gear and here he is now fighting the big fight (whatever that means for your story). In the Climax, we see him face down the antagonist on the page/screen. We don't hear about it later. We see it in the moment as it happens.

Examples of Climax:

Moana: In her boat alone, Moana faces Te Ka in an attempt to get to Te Fiti and return the heart. Te Ka though sends a wave over her boat, knocking it over. As Te Ka is about to blast Moana with fire, Maui returns, risking his hook to help Moana. Moana makes it past Te Ka to where Te Fiti should be. Only to discover that Te Ka is Te Fiti minus her heart. Moana faces the angry fire goddess and returns her heart to her.

Star Wars: Episode IV - A New Hope: Han and Chewie arrive to help Luke. Luke turns off the computer and uses the force to blow up the Death Star.

The Wonderful Wizard of Oz by L. Frank Baum: Because Dorothy is such a passive protagonist in the book, most of the action in the climax is done by other characters while trying to save her. Dorothy does though deliver the final blow when she tries to save the scarecrow from burning and douses the witch with water, melting her. Our passive heroine gets credit for saving the day. However, she does redeem herself a bit later when she discovers the Wizard deceived them and stands up to him. (Our passive protagonist is evolving some.) This is followed by a second Crisis when the Wizard's balloon which was supposed to take them back to Kansas takes off without them.

12.) Resolution/Denouement

Whew. That was a tough fight, but now it is over and it's time to see the outcome. In most stories, this will be triumphant. He won! In a tragedy, not so much. But either way, give us a peek at how things are now. (Maybe even book end with a scene similar to what you showed in the Ordinary World scene to really highlight how your character has changed or not changed.)

Examples of Resolution/Denouement:

Moana: Te Fiti forgives Maui and returns his hook to him. Moana's boat is also restored and returned to her. We see that the blight has left the land. The ocean then rewards her with a shell which she places on the stone pillar as her mark as her people's new leader. Moana has achieved her dream of adventure and brought the gift of sailing back to her people. We see both as they once again sail across the ocean.

Star Wars: Episode IV - A New Hope: Luke, Han, and Chewbacca receive medals from Princess Leia. We see the droids refreshed and new looking.

The Wonderful Wizard of Oz by L. Frank Baum: (Movie) Glinda reveals Dorothy had the power within her to get herself home all the time. Dorothy clicks her heels together and then wakes up back in her bed in Kansas.

These are the 12 steps I use. As you can see there are scenes not mentioned here that you will want to include too. Things like the "Acceptance of the Call" and the scene between the Dark Moment and Climax where something happens that kicks your protagonist back into gear to go face down the antagonist in the Climax.

Why don't I include these in plotting? Because these are scenes that will most likely flow once you have these 12 steps worked out. If they don't for you, or you are afraid you are going to somehow forget, add them during the plotting stage. (Again, check the Bonus section of this book for more scenes you may want to add.)

Chapter Nine:

Here in the Real World
(Building Your Plot)

In Chapter Eight, I introduced you to the **12-step method** that I use for plotting. However, I have found that for many people trying to fill in those twelve steps cold can be intimidating. So we're going to work up to it.

You know your characters (Chapters 1-4), and you have your major goal (Chapter 5), motivation (Chapter 6), and conflict (Chapter 6) for the book. This is huge, but honestly, it isn't enough. It may feel like enough. You may think, "I'm good. I'm going to just start writing." And you can, but odds are good that you will write happily for three chapters or so and hit a wall.

Hard.

You'll think, "I just need to keep writing." And you will. And you will write crap and you will think, "That's okay. You have to write crap... or so I've been told." And you'll keep going and going and... ugh. What a mess.

Or is that just me?

I don't think it is. I think it's a lot of us. And while I am not here to tell you that by using my method you will never write crap or even that writing some crap is *bad*, I *am* here to tell you there is a better way.

And to help you find it.

So let's write down what you have again.

Character Name:

Goal:

Motivation:

Conflict:

Now think back to that motivation. Remember in Chapter 6 when I mentioned you might see that motivation in scene? What was the scene you had in mind?

Motivation Scene:

Oh my gosh… we have our first scene in our book! That was easy.

What else… oh yeah, goal. Your motivation scene may or may not reveal your character's story goal. If it does, great… two must-haves for one scene. You might, though, show the motivation… mother dissing the daughter's achievements at a party for example. Then *later* the daughter, our protagonist, hears that the long-time star of some long-time running Broadway play is retiring, and there is going to be a contest to fill the spot. That news is what sets our character on her path to achieve her main external goal of winning this contest and getting the role. This is her *Inciting Incident* and her mother dissing her is sadly her *Ordinary World*.

In *Star Wars: Episode IV - A New Hope*, Luke's goal is to bring down the Empire. His motivation for this is multi-faceted, but we see a couple of aspects in scene when we experience his Ordinary World, hear how he wants adventure and see his aunt, uncle, and Obi Wan each talking about his father. We then see his biggest motivation, when he returns to his farm to discover that his family and their farm have been destroyed by Storm Troopers (the Empire).

The message here is that you want to show your character's motivation if you can and a great place to do that is in Ordinary World. Something in the world as they know it right now isn't everything it could be... that is their motivation for going on the journey the Inciting Incident will open up for them.

Examples of Ordinary Worlds:

Bridget Jones Diary: Bridget on New Year's Day headed to her "mother's annual turkey curry buffet."

Examples of Inciting Incidents:

Bridget Jones Diary: Bridget overhears Mark Darcy insulting her.

So two plot points/scenes done! Great, but let's not get too excited yet. You are probably somewhere in the first three chapters of your book... still a lot more to go.

So where next?

You may be tempted to go chronologically as in "what happens next."

Don't.

Doing that at this point will make for boring "and then" stuff that isn't going to get us to the big moments that you need or a plot that moves.

So what's your ending? Not the very end where everything is either happy or lost. Right before that. The *big* moment when your protagonist faces down his antagonist. This is your story's and your character's climax. It's what we've been waiting for...!

Examples of Climaxes:

Bridget Jones Diary: Bridget's mother tells her Daniel had the affair with Mark's wife. Realizing her mistake, Bridget rushes to Mark's parents to make things right. She reveals her true feelings/self in front of everyone.

Moana: Moana faces Te Ka alone.

What is the big moment for your story and character? Who does your protagonist have to face down to fully develop or to finish his journey?

Write that down and **make it event**, meaning a scene. *She stands up to her mother in front of everyone, publicly rejecting the goals her mother forced upon her.* This is the moment to show your character's strength, to show her finally facing her fear.

At The End (*Climax*):

Now you have at least three plot points of our goal of twelve done. There is, though, a whole bunch of book between these three and that bunch is the easiest part to get lost in… the part that can easily become the "sagging middle." We don't want our middles to sag, so let's keep going.

The following illustration shows where we would be if we didn't keep going… a book with a big percentage of Ordinary World followed by an Inciting Incident then a sagging middle and a Climax. Also, a book that wouldn't keep many readers reading all the way to that Climax.

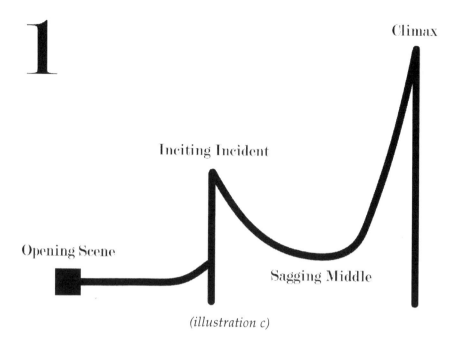

(illustration c)

The next question I want you to ask yourself is…What could happen in the middle of your story that would completely change the trajectory of where your character is going? Another way to think of this is an end to one story and the kick off of another, something that big. This, the *Midpoint*, is where things change so drastically the hero cannot go back to that Ordinary World even if he wants to. All chips are in. He **HAS** to go forward.

The character's fear will be the same, and he still won't have his core need met, but his external goal may change or his method for getting to that external goal may change so drastically it is like a new story in many ways.

At the *Midpoint* your character might:
 -Have something wonderful or horrible happen.
 -Have a secret revealed, to or about them.
 -Get some new information that changes their perspective.

They may also at this moment take what author James Scott Bell calls a "mirror moment." It's that moment when the character realizes what he has become or what he has to do and reflects on it. This reflection will propel them to do something different. In *Gone with the Wind*, it's when Scarlett realizes that Tara is a risk and she is the only person left who can save it. In *Casablanca*, it's where after Rick Blaine's lost love, Ilsa, speaks with him and Rick lashes out, when he is forced to question what kind of man he has become.

Whatever happens at the mid-point though, it has to change things. It will push your character to go in a new direction or even feel like the beginning of a whole new story.

Examples of Midpoints:

The Wizard of Oz: Dorothy arrives at the Emerald City
Star Wars: Princess Leia is rescued and the group escapes to the Rebel base.
Bridget Jones Diary: In response to Daniel's infidelity, Bridget quits her job in spectacular fashion.

With our Broadway play, our character starts off trying to win the contest, get the role, and please her mother. We (or I at least) have been assuming that her friend's plans for the dog rescue are known fairly early on too; it is our major conflict with her external goal. But what if in the beginning, our character is more focused on the Broadway play and the dog rescue thing is just there, kind of getting in her way. What if though, somewhere in the middle of the book, something happens where our character has to change what she is doing completely?

Do some brainstorming. Make a list. Be crazy. Be bold. Then, eventually, pick one.

Maybe it will work. Maybe it won't. The beauty of plotting is, hopefully, we will find out before writing 100,000 words.

So, for our dog and theatre loving protagonist what could happen?

-Her friend could be arrested, leaving all the dogs uncared for.

-Her mother could die, zapping her will to continue with her goal.

-She could discover the producer of the play is an animal hoarder.

-She could discover the play was a front for prostitution.

As you can see, some of these would take us way off our original plan for this book. We are writing a story of self-discovery and strength. We don't want to get weighed down with police investigations or lose the mother who is our motivation. Who would our protagonist stand up to in the end then?

In general, I'm not a fan of what feels like a coincidence which her friend wanting to do animal rescue and the producer being an animal hoarder feels like, but I think we can work around that, so it isn't a coincidence. We're writers... and we still haven't actually written anything, remember? Maybe the friend is how our protagonist learned of the contest. This friend knows the producer from the animal world but doesn't know her dark animal-hoarding secret, etc.

So now our protagonist learns the producer is an animal hoarder. If she turns her in, the woman will be tied up in court, get tons of bad publicity, and the contest will be dropped or at least put off indefinitely. This new information changes everything. Now our protagonist can't just go to rehearsals like everyone else. She has to do something. Save the animals. Keep her friend from reporting the producer. Keep the contest on track.

In this case, she still has her overall goal, but the focus has definitely shifted.

In Stage 2, you see our new Midpoint helping to prop up our sagging middle. We aren't there complete plot-wise, but getting there...

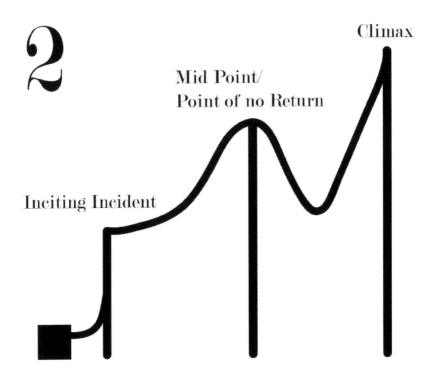

(illustration c)

So, for your book, what is it? What is the **Point of No Return** for your character? What changes everything for him or her so he can't go back to who they were or the world they knew at the begging of the book? Be bold. (Remember this is just plotting, if it doesn't work, you can change it.)

Midpoint/Point of No Return:

Got that? Or a starting idea at least?

Okay, now we are ready if you can take it, to move on to the final stage, stage 3.

Illustration c looks a lot better than illustration b, but there is still a lot of potential between those tent poles for our story to drag and sag. Let's try to prop everything up a bit more.

Let's add a scene where the *Protagonist Engages,* where he or she does something to make the story move along. The lack of this kind of scene is one of the plotting issues I see most often with first manuscripts.

And I get it.

It can be tempting to let events push your protagonist along. Bad things happen to him; he reacts. Maybe **lots** of bad things happen.

Isn't that enough?

No, it isn't. Strangely, this too, like that sagging middle, makes for a boring read.

You want to write about a protagonist who people root for, and guess what?

Readers root for characters who are active-who try to control their own destiny, not just be pushed along like a leaf in a stream.

(Side note: You may be thinking, but what about Dorothy? What about Luke Skywalker in the first Star Wars movie? They weren't incredibly active. You told us that yourself.... Yes, this is true, but both of those examples had a couple of things in common. First, they both had ensemble casts all working towards the same general goal. So if the hero was a bit blah in his actions, there was someone else to be strong. Also, both of these movies are a bit, dare I say... old. Viewers and readers tastes do change and today readers and viewers lean towards more active protagonists. But back to that "First," someone has to be active and I highly suggest in today's world, you make it your protagonist.)

So, in the first quarter to third of your book, your hero needs to engage (for the first time. He needs to keep engaging as the story goes on too). But here, *in the beginning somewhere,* he needs to say, "I'm going to do something about this."

His choice of action can be all wrong, and he can and should get slapped back down by the antagonist, but he has to decide to jump into the fight, whatever that fight may be.

In our contest for the Broadway play, this can be as simple as our protagonist going and entering the contest. That is her engaging. It is your protagonist deciding to take up "the call" to address whatever issue was brought up in the *Inciting Incident* and the reader seeing that in scene. But make her do it. Make her decide she is taking this action on. Don't just have her *be there*. Make her own it.

Examples of Protagonist Engages:

Bridget Jones Diary: Bridget goes after Daniel Cleaver (working against the goal she had just set for herself)

Have that? Write it down and put it between the *Inciting Incident* and the *Midpoint*.

Protagonist engages by...

Then go to the end. You have this beautiful *Climax* all thought out and you can't wait to get your protagonist to that point. But if he gets there too easily, your reader just won't care. We readers are a mean bunch. We like to see characters at their depths and the lower we see them, the bigger their victory will seem. So give us a *Dark Moment*.

The *Dark Moment* is the place where your character thinks everything is lost–where there is no way he can win this fight, and he sits down for a bit and eats a few worms. Why bother? He is going to lose anyway.

Examples of Dark Moment:

Bridget Jones Diary: Mark has left and Bridget has walked away from Daniel. She has lost everything. (and she did it to herself) She winds up back at her parents, in her pajamas while they get ready to go out for New Year's Eve.

In our contest for the Broadway play role, this could be the point where our protagonist is forced to face that she can't be a good person, save the dogs AND win the contest. Maybe she is offered the win, but only if she ignores the dog hoarding. Maybe she actually turns her back on something bad happening to those dogs because of her desire to win the contest.

How would this make her feel about herself?

If she is someone we would like, she'd feel bad… very, very bad.

Her dream or the dogs? She can't have both.

In the *Dark Moment*, we want to see the after-effects of realizing she has failed. We want to see her break down, shove her friends away who are trying to congratulate her. See her drinking or cussing or doing whatever this character would do when forced to face the realities of her choice. We want to see her at her very bottom.

What is this for your character in your story? Write it down.

Dark Moment:

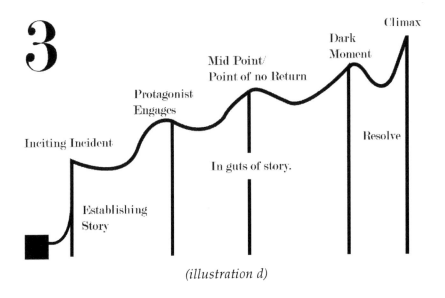

(illustration d)

And with that, you have a plot with highs and lows. A plot with no sagging middle that shows the bit before your protagonist starts on his/her journey (*Ordinary World*), where he is introduced to a choice (*Inciting Incident*), where he goes for his goal (*Protagonist Engages*), where he is so deep into his journey that there is no road back to who he was (*Midpoint/Point of No Return*), where he knows all is lost and acts on the knowledge that he can't have it all and will have to make an impossible choice (*Dark Moment*), and finally, when your protagonist rallies, where he makes that hard choice and takes on the antagonist/final challenge in scene (*Climax*).

You have a story.

Let's recap.

If you've been playing along you now know your main characters' cloak/mask, fear, strength that he uses as a crutch to hide his fear, his motto, the characteristic that he admires most in others and that is hopefully hidden within him somewhere, his weakness that gets him in trouble with the antagonist, his dark side, his core need, and his true and happy self.

Using this information, you were able to establish his internal goal and his external goal.

From this, you found the main external goal which will drive your plot, the character's motivation for that goal, and the main conflict that stops him from easily achieving that goal.

You also have at least four to six key scenes that keep your story moving and take the reader on emotional highs and lows, that keep your reader reading.

Should we stop?

Nah, not yet.

Form: Finding your Plot Points and more

At the beginning of your book, how is your character's world? How is your character? Give us a brief sketch or scene that shows his/her outlook on life. (*Ordinary World-Plot Point 1*)

What does your character want? (External Goal)

How do we see this? (*Inciting Incident – Plot Point 2*)

What happens that makes achieving this goal more important than it ever has been? (*Raise the Stakes/ Plot Point 3*)

How does your character react to the above problem? What are some choices he could make that seem "smart/good?"

How could these choices make things harder for the antagonist?

What could the antagonist do to lessen the effect of these choices on them?

Based on previous three questions, what events could happen? (Scene cards for each.)

Chapter Ten:

You've Never Been This Way Before
(Finishing Your Plot)

Now that you have the basics down, let's flesh things out a bit. To do this, I'm going to give you some questions to answer.

Hint: you should already know some of this from our previous work in this book.

Pro Tip: Anything labeled with a Plot Point or "scene," write the answers on index cards to use later when you are ready to actually start writing.

Protagonist does…?

Antagonist does…?

At what point does your main character decide the problem is important enough that he has to deal with it? (*Protagonist Engages – Plot Point 4*)

Refer back to your goal/conflict work. What is in the way of your character reaching his/her goal?

What at this point in the story would the antagonist do that would get in the way of your character reaching his goal? (*Antagonist Bites Back – Plot Point 5*)

What could happen to change everything your character believes? List three things.

1.)

2.)

3.)

Pick one of above and describe how it would look in scene. Things have changed so much for your character that he cannot go back to how things were at the beginning. He can't just walk away and act like nothing has happened. Show us. (*Point of No Return/Midpoint – Plot Point 6*)

Your character is all set and working hard towards his new goal or a new take on the old one. What is something that could get in his way? Some event that we could see that would make things harder for him? (*Pinch/Tighten the Screw – Plot Point 7*)

What is the absolute worst thing that could happen to your character? Something that would make your character walk away from their goal? List three things.

1.)

2.)

3.)

Pick one and tell us how this would look in scene. (*Crisis – Plot Point 9*)

Now go back a bit... what could your character have done that would have CAUSED this crisis? Nothing? Completely out of his control? Then go back, pick a different crisis until you have one he could have in some way brought onto himself. Have that? GREAT. Now tell us what he did that brought this crisis to reality: *(Turning Point to Crisis - Plot Point 8)*

The crisis was tough. Now imagine your character has given up. What would he do in total defeat? How would he react? List three possible scenarios. Include emotions.

1.)

2.)

3.)

Pick one and tell us how this would look in scene. *(Dark Moment - Plot Point 10)*

What could make your character rise again? What would motivate him to get back up and continue the fight? List three things.

1.)

2.)

3.)

What would the antagonist do to stop your character from reaching his/her goal?

1.)

2.)

3.)

How might these two face off, in the same space/time over this goal? (Think big.)

The antagonist wins. How does this look for your character and the antagonist?

The character wins. How does this look for your character and the antagonist?

Pick one of the above scenarios and describe it in scene. (*Climax – Plot Point 11*)

The battle has ended. How does your character's world look now? How has your character changed or not changed? Show us in scene. (*Resolution/Denouement Plot Point 12*)

Got all of that?

Then you, my friend, have plotted your book.

Take a minute. Look through your cards. Go through some of the options you came up when answering these questions, add some of those to cards. Shuffle the cards, rearrange them, toss some, check out the bonus section of this book… and then?

Start writing.

~~~

Thanks so much for reading *Hello, Plot. Are You Out There?* I sincerely hope that it will help you connect character and plot in your books and make plotting future projects both more fun and easier.

If you do find it useful, please leave a review or recommend it to your writing friends.

For more information on all things writing, please visit my writing website The How To Write Shop. It is full of free articles on the craft and business of writing.

Also, checkout The How To Write Shop on Facebook and Twitter.

Keep reading, there's more information and a link to get the *Hello, Plot. Workbook.*

Thanks!

Lori

Hello Plot Workbook in PDF

Get your copy here:

https://bookhip.com/VJDMSL

Extras –

Then You Can Tell Me Goodbye

Other scenes

This is a list of additional scenes to those outlined in the 12 Plot Points that you may want to add to your story. Not all are needed for every story.

Some may be already covered in your 12 Plot Points. Some are just a slight twist on what I listed or even more of a technique to enhance a scene rather than a full-blown scene on their own. And some you may include naturally as you fill in between the 12 Points.

But I think they all deserve an extra mention. Use what you will...

Call to Adventure-

Call to Adventure comes from the Hero's Journey. However, even if you aren't following the entire Hero's Journey it is one of the scenes from that method that you may want to consider including. It may be the same as your Inciting Incident, or it may come soon after. It is the scene where someone or something calls the protagonist to change his path, to embark on a new journey.

He found the body (Inciting Incident), but it didn't really involve him. The police take care of that kind of thing. But then his best friend is brought in for questioning and asks him to follow up on a few things...

Refusal of the Call

Another step in the Hero's Journey, the Refusal of the Call is simply when the protagonist says... "No, I'm good. I'll just keep doing what I'm doing." This may be because they are reluctant to get involved or it may be because they think they aren't worthy. Whatever the reason, they try to stick with their Ordinary World.

Departure or Crossing the First Threshold

This is yet another Hero's Journey step. This is the scene where we see that our protagonist is entering a new world. Harry Potter finds platform 9.75 and gets on the train. In *Silence of the Lambs*, Clarice Starling enters the prison where Hannibal Lector is being held. This scene solidifies for the view or reader that things have changed and are about to change more. They are on the ride.

Change of Plans-

Also called a Reversal scene, a Change of Plans scene is when your character enters the scene with one goal or motivation and something happens that changes everything. Usually, you will see these in the last third of a book. In *Casablanca,* we know Rick Blaine loves Ilsa. We also know that Ilsa plans on going with Rick. But when the big moment comes, when Rick has what we know he wants in his grasp, he instead puts her on that plane with her husband. In *Silence of the Lambs,* we are told the FBI has found Buffalo Bill and are on their way to arrest him. We see Buffalo Bill going about his business in his house. We see the FBI approaching the house, and we also see Clarice approaching what is supposed to be a different house. Then, bam, Buffalo Bill opens the door to Clarice. (Reversal part one). Clarice enters with a simple goal to gather more information until she notices a few clues that make her realize she has landed in the house of the killer, and she has an abrupt Change of Plans. (Reversal part two)

Meet with the Mentor

In the Hero's Journey, this is also called Supernatural Aid, and the aid may include items such as weapons or talismans. However, in most of today's stories, the aid isn't supernatural at all, and the aid is more advice than item.

It's usually talking with a best friend, or a boss, or even some smart-aleck kid who sees things more clearly than your protagonist does. This scene gives your character someone to talk things out with rather than sitting in a room by himself musing.

Your protagonist may have more than one character who acts as a mentor, but you don't necessarily want multiple scenes dedicated to mainly this. The nature of talking tends to make them a bit slow... unless you utilize another trick Pope in the Pool.

Pope in the Pool

This scene comes from *Save the Cat* by Blake Snyder. It isn't a scene by itself so much as a technique to make an otherwise boring scene more interesting. The name and idea came from a movie where there was a scene where a lot of boring information needed to be relayed to the viewer. Instead of having the parties involved sit and meet at a coffee shop or diner, this smart screenwriter put them at a pool with the Pope swimming. As Snyder points out, the uniqueness of seeing the Pope in swim trunks paddling around was enough to bring life to what could have been a very dull bit. So if you find yourself needing to write an information-driven scene, think can you put the Pope in a pool? (A version of the Pope and pool appropriate to your story, of course.)

Mirror Moment-

Mirror moment comes from James Scott Bell, but you can also call this sequel (Dwight V. Swain) or reflection. If you followed my 12 Plot Points, you already have one scene such as this with your Dark Moment.

A reflection scene is when your character takes a moment to look at himself- what he is or what he has become. This moment with the mirror should motivate him to do something different. It should lead to a new event or scene.

Do you need this in your book? Yes and no. Mirror moments show motivation. And you do need to show motivation. They show your character making a realization and prepping themselves to do something different on the page. Showing this will keep readers from feeling that something was "out of character." The question becomes how long this moment needs to be. I think at least one strong moment, like the Dark Moment, is important and perhaps another at the midpoint (where Bell pinpoints Mirror Moments as occurring), but you can also just show the reader this in as little as a couple of lines. (sequel)

Save the Cat

Like Pope in the Pool, Save the Cat comes from *Save the Cat* by Blake Snyder. This is also inspired by a movie scene where the bad guy goes back into a burning building to literally "save the cat." What purpose does this serve? To make the antagonist or any character more human and more likable. And, no, you don't have to have a cat for your character to save. He doesn't have to actually *save* anything. The point of a Save the Cat scene or moment is to give an otherwise unlikable character some redeeming quality that makes readers if not *like* him, at least understand that he isn't *all* bad.

~~~

Mystery Specific:

There's A Body-

Someone died. We want to see it.

We don't have to see the murder happen (although that is an option); we could see the discovery. One of these things is most likely the Inciting Incident in a murder mystery, but I have seen writers try to write a murder mystery novel where the body had been discovered and the reader never sees it. This feels like a rip-off or author copout... so give us at least one: the murder itself, or the discovery of the body.

Possible exceptions? Of course. Some pulp fiction detective novels start with the mysterious client coming to see the detective. Maybe you can make this work, but still consider showing us that body, dying or dead.

Make it Personal

One of the big challenges when writing a mystery is making the goal personal. Usually, the obvious external goal is to catch the killer. But if that is it, if catching the killer is just a job or a hobby and there is nothing personal driving anything in the novel, the plot will lack umph and your readers will lack enthusiasm.

So, make it personal. **Without a big backstory dump.**

This can be done in a couple of ways. First is a Make it Personal scene where you show us something that makes finding this killer important and personal to our detective. Maybe this detective was in charge of watching the child who was kidnapped. Maybe this detective has a child of the same age. You don't have to smack us over the head with what the personal is but do show it to us.

There are other options for this. You may be able to just sneak a line in here and there that relays this fine in another type of scene or you may have a mystery where some other plotline (that is personal) is actually driving the book and the mystery is just there adding color, but then, is it a mystery? Really?

Red Herrings

A Red Herring alone probably isn't enough to carry a whole scene, but you do need red herrings in your mystery novel. So, making notes to remind yourself where you are placing them is a good double check.

Wrong Conclusions

You can easily have an entire scene dedicated to a wrong conclusion. Your detective has been following up on those Red Herrings that you have scattered about, and now he knows the answer. He has captured the killer. All is well. Except it isn't. He fingered the wrong guy. (This could also be a Pinch, Crisis, or Reversal scene.)

The Big Reveal

Remember these? Ah, Poirot, how we love you. This scene is part of the Climax. Your detective sits all the involved or potentially involved parties down and sets out everything he has discovered. The beauty of this old school scene is it keeps you from having to clear up all the details of what happened after the Climax in the Resolution/Denouement. (In today's world you may need to spice this up though with a little Pope in the Pool…)

~~~

Romance Specific:

First Meet

This is just what it sounds like: the hero and heroine meet on the pages of the book. This can be the "first" meet or it can be a "re" meet. But we have to see that face to face interaction. Until this happens the reader won't know for sure that the romance plot has really started. This meet can be what we call a "cute" meet. This is something like the heroine's dog sneaks into the hero's house and escapes with his boxer shorts. The heroine is then caught by the hero trying to hide the evidence. Or it can be dramatic: hero is shot, and heroine is the police officer who arrives at the crime scene.

The meet scene, however, has to have the elements of attraction and conflict. Right off the bat, we (the readers) want to see that these people are attracted to each other, but that their pairing is not going to come easy.

Look What We Share

We ended the meet with conflict. Now we want to show that the pair has something in common beyond the surface attraction they showed in the meet. Going back to our boxer-short stealing dog, maybe the dog after its extensive diet of undergarments gets sick. While the heroine is panicking trying to get her pet into the car to take it to the vet, along comes the hero who we learn has a strange way with dogs and gets the boxer-eater safely in the vehicle for transport.

Alas though, this scene can't end all happy. Since all scenes must end in either conflict or questions raised, our heroine is going to resent something about how the hero conducted himself. Perhaps he raised an eyebrow at Fido's tutu or suggested Fido could drop a few pounds. At this point too, if you haven't already, you need to add the overall big conflict between them. Maybe our hero is on the condo board and was actually searching our heroine out to give her notice that Fido is a violation of the building's no dog policy.

In the reader's mind, we have established that these people share more than just a physical attraction, but the conflict keeping them apart is even bigger than originally thought. (Or as big as originally thought if the major conflict was established in the meet.)

(It is also important, of course, to give the hero a good motivation as to why he can't just ignore the rules, but let's just say for now that you have done that and relayed it to the reader.)

Physical Attraction

We got a peek at this in the meet and you should have been showing this in all the hero/heroine interactions to some degree, but at some point, you have to really show this on the page with a kiss or some other physical act. Whether you choose a kiss or a full-blown sex scene, remember these acts change things for the characters. The conflict that is keeping our hero/heroine apart is still there, but they kissed! What caused that? What to do now?

This physical act should be a new source of conflict, at least internal conflict.

Emotional Commitment

You may think your readers have figured out that your characters love each other, but when writing romance, you have to show it on the page. You have to have one or both characters admit it on the page. This can be to the other character or in inner monologue, but it needs to be declared.

Sacrifice for Love

Remember that story conflict? Well, it hasn't gone away, and it shouldn't. Someone, in the end, needs to make a choice between the conflict and love for the other character. Someone has to give something up – even better, both characters need to give something up. This is how they change or arc. At the beginning of the book if presented with the choice of love or whatever this other thing represented by the conflict is, they would have chosen the conflict. But now? Not a chance.

Intro to the Hero's Journey

In his book, *The Hero with a Thousand Faces*, American mythologist, and author, Joseph Campbell introduced us to the idea of *The Hero's Journey*. This "journey" describes basic stages that heroes in quest-type stories go through in tales told across the world and for generations.

The patterns found in these stories are so consistent and so ancient, Campbell believed that they called out to something deep within all of us, something universal and never-changing.

His ideas of the hero and the characters that the hero encounters correspond with the teachings of Carl Jung. Both see archetypes in quest stories, characters who reoccur in dreams, stories, and myths. Jung believed that these archetypes were part of our "collective unconscious."

This is why stories that follow *The Hero's Journey* with the quest archetypes have such power to grab readers and viewers. They are speaking to something basic and universal.

If you want to go to the original source, read *The Hero with a Thousand Faces* and check out the documentary that Campbell did with Bill Moyers, *The Power of Myth*.

You may also want to check out (or just go straight to) *The Writer's Journey* by Christopher Vogler. Vogler takes Campbell's *Hero's Journey* and simplifies it for writers.

Or you can just read my brief breakdown that follows… or maybe all of the above.

Note: When you research the Hero's Journey or any of the plotting structures based on it, you will find the same general ideas called many different things. As Shakespeare would tell you, names don't matter. Look at what the stage actually shows and decide if it is right for your story. You may want to skip some. You may also want to move some. Use the Hero's or Writer's or whatever other Journey as a guide, not a law.

You will also see that The Hero's Journey has more steps with more symbolism than The Writer's Journey or other plotting structures. For some stories, it can be a lot of fun to try and work these in. For example, can you think of a Belly of the Whale scene? Or a Magic Flight? If you can and it adds to your story, give it a try, but don't force things. Use what works for you and your story.

Stage One (Act One in a Three-Act Structure): Departure

Ordinary World

Life as character knows it before the adventure begins. Often only a small slice of this is shown in modern genre fiction — or not at all. (Star Wars: Luke on the farm.)

The Call to Adventure

When the character is first notified everything is about to change. (Star Wars: Obi-Wan "You must come with me to Alderaan")

Refusal of the Call

Just what the title says. The character's first reaction is "no, not me." (Star Wars: Luke says "No, I'm staying on the farm.")

Supernatural Aid

After character commits to journey a mentor or aid appears. This meet with the mentor also might be what gives the character a nudge to commit to the journey. (Star Wars: Obi-Wan and to some degree droids.)

The Crossing of the First Threshold

The character actually enters the new world created by taking the call. Shows the reader that the main character is somewhere new/away from the ordinary world. (Star Wars: Mos Eisley spaceport and the cantina.)

The Belly of the Whale

Point where the character is transitioning between two worlds (ordinary and new) and two selves (before changes needed to succeed at the journey and after). Often symbolized as something dark and scary...like being trapped in the belly of a whale. Character shows at this point that he is ready to die (at least let his old self die). (Star Wars: the trash compactor.)

Stage Two (Act Two in a Three-Act Structure): Initiation

The Road of Trials

Series of tests, tasks, or ordeals that the character has to get through to begin the transformation that he came to grips with in the Belly of The Whale. The character often fails at one or more of these tasks...he is learning to become a character capable of ending the journey victorious. (Star Wars: events leading to the destruction of Death Star and rescue of Princess Leia.)

The Meeting with the Goddess

Point where the character experiences a love that is powerful and significant, like the love of a mother or the mother goddess. This may take place within the character—a marriage of sorts of his two halves, spiritual and physical or this may be represented by the character loving another character in this all-encompassing way. (Unconditional love and/or self-unification) (Star Wars: Luke's feelings for Princess Leia.)

Woman as the Temptress

Does not have to be a woman, but something that represents the hero's need to step away from his physical/earthy needs. This is, however, often shown with a woman, the lust the hero feels for her, and his own disgust over this lust that could pull him away from his journey. (Star Wars: Princess Leia is both Goddess and Temptress.)

Atonement with the Father

This is the midpoint in the journey. The character confronts whatever holds the most power in his life. (Takes on the father as a step into manhood.) Everything has led us to this point. It is where the character proves he is capable of going on alone. Character's old self dies at this point, sometimes literally. (Star Wars: Luke puts aside the computer and lets the force lead him.)

Apotheosis

Point of divine knowledge after death. In modern fiction short this is a period of peace and fulfillment before the character begins the final stage of the journey. (Star Wars: Luke's high after putting aside the computer.)

The Ultimate Boon

Achievement of the goal of the journey. (Star Wars: Things look bad for the Death Star and Luke understands the ways of the Force.)

Stage Three (Act Three in a Three-Act Structure): Return

Refusal of the Return

The character may not want to return from the journey. He may think of staying in this new place.

The Magic Flight

The character may have to escape with the "boon" while others give chase. (Star Wars: Luke is chased by Millennium Falcon.)

Rescue from Without

Guide or assistant who helps bring the character back to the world or convinces them they need to bring the "boon" to the world. (Star Wars: Hans Solo returns to save Luke from being blown up.)

The Crossing of the Return Threshold

The character returns to the old world, often to find it changed. Getting "boon" to work for this world may prove difficult. (Star Wars: We don't see Luke return to his original world, the farm, but we know this world has changed from earlier scene where the farm was destroyed. We do see Luke return to the rebel base, his new world.)

Master of the Two Worlds

Character gets to a place of balance between spiritual and physical worlds (or inner and outer worlds). (Star Wars: Luke is star pilot but can also use the Force.)

Freedom to Live

The character is master of his own destiny, capable of living in the moment, free from fear of death and doesn't regret the past or worry about the future.

Extra Forms

Form: Getting More from your Antagonist

Name:

What does your antagonist fear?

Does this fear have any similarities to what your protagonist fears?

Does your antagonist have any other similarities to your protagonist?

Could your antagonist be a doppelganger antagonist? (Your protagonist's dark side.)

To hide his fear/doubt from others, what action might your antagonist take?

What strength do they have that will help them hide their fear/doubt?

What internal dialogue might they have to justify this fear/doubt?

What is your antagonist's redeeming characteristic?

For each of the above list a scene where the reader sees these things. (Can also repeat all steps you went through for your protagonist.)

Now let's check to see if your antagonist is pulling his/her weight...

What is your main antagonist's goal? (hint if he gets what he wants, your protagonist won't get what he wants – or it will seem impossible for both to get what they want)

What are five things your antagonist would do to get what he wants? Think event.

For each above event, list something that could stop the antagonist from completing that event.

Is there anywhere in your book that you don't (as the author) know what your antagonist is doing or thinking?

During the above, what is the antagonist doing/thinking?

Don't forget to make the Antagonist real.

Write a short paragraph from the antagonist's point of view on why he HAS to do the things he does in your story. Why is his cause the right one? Make this real and heartfelt.

What justification could you find for the antagonist's case from a political, religious, philosophical, or another widely held belief angle?

Who in your story is on the antagonist's side or would side with the antagonist if given the opportunity to hear his/her side of things? Write a short paragraph where this character argues his/her case.

Now write a paragraph where your protagonist realizes the antagonist is right.

Where could you use these paragraphs (or variations of them)?

Bibliography & Information of Possible Further Interest

Bell, James Scott. "James Scott Bell: The 'Write From The Middle' Method." Writers Helping Writers, 12 Mar. 2014, writershelpingwriters.net/2014/03/james-scott-bell-write-middle-method/.

"Enneagram Worldwide." Enneagram Studies in the Narrative Tradition, www.enneagramworldwide.com.

"Home." The Enneagram Institute, www.enneagraminstitute.com.

Searle, Judith. The Literary Enneagram: Characters from the inside Out. Ignudo Press, 2011.

Snyder, Blake. Save the Cat!: The Last Book on Screenwriting That You'll Ever Need. Michael Wiese Productions, 2005.

Swain, Dwight V. Techniques of the Selling Writer. Univ. Oklahoma P., 1981.

Vogler, Christopher. The Writer's Journey: Mythic Structure for Storytellers and Screenwriter's. Wiese, 2008.

And, of course, www.HowToWriteShop.com

19710436R00087

Made in the USA
Lexington, KY
29 November 2018